D1175994

Liquidity Preferences
of Commercial
Banks

This volume is a publication of the
Workshop in Money and Banking

*

ECONOMICS RESEARCH STUDIES

of the

ECONOMICS RESEARCH CENTER

of the

UNIVERSITY OF CHICAGO

Liquidity Preferences of Commercial Banks

By

GEORGE R. MORRISON

THE UNIVERSITY OF CHICAGO PRESS

CHICAGO & LONDON

Library of Congress Catalog Card Number: 66-13882

THE UNIVERSITY OF CHICAGO PRESS, CHICAGO & LONDON
The University of Toronto Press, Toronto 5, Canada

© *1966 by The University of Chicago. All rights reserved*
Published 1966. Second Impression 1967

Printed in the United States of America

332./2
MＪ79L
/69458

Acknowledgments

An earlier version of this study was presented as my doctoral dissertation to the Department of Economics at the University of Chicago in March, 1963.

During the course of this study, I received financial aid in the form of fellowships and funds for research assistance from the Federal Reserve Bank of St. Louis, the American Bankers Association, and the Money and Banking Workshop of the University of Chicago.

My thanks for helpful comments on previous drafts of the study are due to Haskel Benishay, Phillip Cagan, William Dewald, Frank DeLeeuw, Homer Jones, A. James Meigs, and to Harry G. Johnson and Reuben Kessel, who served as members of my thesis committee. I have benefited by discussions with economists too numerous to mention during my periods of association with the Money and Banking Workshop, the economic research staffs of the Federal Reserve Bank of St. Louis, and the Board of Governors of the Federal Reserve. My principal debt is to Milton Friedman, who suggested the topic and acted as chairman of my thesis committee.

Lily Monheit of the University of Chicago and Robert Steinberg and M. Herbert Schwartz of the Board of Governors of the Federal Reserve supervised the considerable burden of computer work involved in this project.

Above all, I owe my greatest thanks to my wife, Rita, for the many weeks she worked, patiently gathered and computed statistical series, typed and edited manuscript, and offered encouragement. It is a simple fact that the study would not have been completed without her help.

Contents

Figures

Tables

I

Introduction

MONETARY THEORY may usefully be divided into two sections. One section is concerned with expenditure and balance sheet decisions of the public insofar as they evolve from factors influencing the public's desired stock of money. The other section quite naturally concerns itself with forces influencing the actual stock of money. The objective of this study is to investigate a portion of commercial bank behavior that has at times, occupied a critical position among factors influencing fluctuations in the actual money stock, namely, the relation between the cash reserves of banks and their deposit liabilities.

Theories of monetary policy often emphasize the need for centralized control over the money supply. Yet, under modern conditions, at best the central bank has direct control over the reserves of commercial banks. Under a fractional reserve commercial banking system, the ability of a central monetary authority indirectly to control the stock of money with reasonable precision depends in large measure on the short-run stability of the relation between bank reserves and deposits. Even if the central bank has firm control over the volume of commercial bank reserves, this does not automatically assure close central bank control over the volume of bank deposits. The extent to which reserves are used to create deposits is only partly determined by central bank policy. Ordinarily a substantial range of discretion is left to the commercial banks in choosing the amount of deposits they create on the basis of given reserves.

Widespread realization among economists of the significance of the relation of bank reserves to deposits seems to have coincided with the first clear statements of the deposit creation process for individual banks and the banking system, by Phillips and Crick[1] in the 1920's. In their formulations of the multiple by which deposits of the banking system can be created on the basis of a given volume of bank reserves, the multiple is

[1] C. A. Phillips, *Bank Credit* (New York: Macmillan & Co., 1920), pp. 32–76. W. F. Crick, "The Genesis of Bank Deposits," *Economica*, VII (1927), 191–202. Also see J. M. Keynes, *A Treatise on Money* (London: Macmillan & Co., 1930), II, 13, 16–17, 49–66; J. E. Meade, "The Amount of Money and the Banking System," *Economic Journal*, XLIV (1934), 77–83.

simply the reciprocal of the ratio of reserves to deposits that banks in the aggregate desire to maintain.[2]

Economists in the 1920's often took the somewhat sanguine view that the ratio of reserves to deposits desired by banks tended to be relatively constant.[3] According to Phillips: "when the individual bank has become assimilated to the banking system of which it is a part, the ratio of cash to deposits is regulated and kept fairly constant through the banker's control over cash."[4]

Crick was even more adamant on this point and also indicated its implications for central bank policy:

The general stability of cash ratios is too well known to need detailed demonstration. The returns published by the [London clearing] banks are monthly averages of figures taken out on a particular day in each week. Probably the ratio of cash to deposits varies somewhat from day to day; probably too the ratios of which the published figures are averages differ appreciably. We know that the monthly figures vary fractionally, and in the case of some banks at the turn of the half-year, very substantially. Nevertheless, they reveal a degree of steadiness which is obviously much more than accidental.

. . . as a fact, banks rarely change their policies in the matter of cash ratios, and . . . as a matter of record they adhere quite closely to the figures they adopt. It follows that changes in bank cash are the cause of inflationary and deflationary movements.[5]

J. M. Keynes leaned toward this view in his *Treatise on Money:*

. . . at any given time banks stick closely to their established ratio, and . . . such fluctuations as there are exhibit no correlation with the state of trade. This result is what one would expect. To let the ratio fall below the figure which has been fixed . . . would be a sign of weakness or, at least, of weak mindedness; whilst to let it rise above would be to forego quite unnecessarily a source of profit, since surplus reserves can always be employed in the purchase of bills or investments.

Accordingly, the statistics . . . show that, save in exceptional circumstances, all banks use their reserves up to the hilt; that is to say, they seldom or never maintain idle reserves in excess of what is their conventional or legal proportion for the time being.[6]

---

[2] In a fuller treatment, it would be necessary to allow for the effect on the level of deposits of the public's desired ratio of currency to deposits, which will determine, in part, the volume of reserves available to banks for backing deposits.

[3] The formal parallel between the assumed constancy of the desired cash reserve ratio and the assumed constancy of the velocity of money in some of the earlier and less sophisticated versions of the quantity theory will become evident from the model of bank liquidity preference presented in Chapter II.

[4] Phillips, *op. cit.*, p. 79.

[5] Crick, *op. cit.*, pp. 192, 201, 202.   [6] Keynes, *op. cit.*, p. 53.

A similar opinion was expressed by E. A. Goldenweiser of the Federal Reserve Board's economic research staff:

> While member banks do not permit their reserve deposits to fall below the legal limit on account of the penalties for deficient reserves, neither do they carry any considerable amount of excess reserves. Whenever their reserves exceed the legal minimum they find employment for their excess funds either in additional loans or in investments. The ratio of member banks' reserve deposits to their own deposits has, as a matter of fact, remained practically constant at 10 per cent throughout the recent periods of credit expansion and contraction.[7]

The tendency for excess reserves of member banks to constitute a negligible fraction of their total reserves was frequently laid to the ready accessibility for member banks of the Federal Reserve's facilities for discounting eligible paper. Excess reserves were no longer needed for purposes of meeting reserve deficiencies, since the Federal Reserve stood ready to lend member banks reserve funds in case of need. Consequently, during the 1920's, discussions of monetary policy in the United States frequently took for granted the constancy of the excess reserve ratio (at approximately zero) and focused instead on the factors determining the volume of member bank borrowing from the Federal Reserve.[8] Instability

[7] E. A. Goldenweiser, *Federal Reserve System in Operation* (New York: McGraw-Hill Book Co., 1925), pp. 85–86. Also see C. O. Hardy, *Credit Policies of the Federal Reserve System* (Washington: Brookings Institution, 1932), p. 21.

[8] The standard treatment of this problem has been W. W. Riefler, *Money Rates and Money Markets* (New York: Harper & Bros., 1930), which attributed variations in the amount of member bank borrowings to a reluctance on the part of banks to borrow except out of necessities arising from disturbances to their reserve positions. Although some banks may borrow for profit, when the spread between market interest rates and the discount rate is sufficiently wide, the profit motive, according to Riefler, could not have been the dominant factor motivating bank borrowing, else the spread between short-term market rates and the discount rate would not have shown the wide divergences that it did during the 1920's. In Riefler's view, the *spread* between short-term market interest rates and the discount rate does not explain the level of borrowings; rather, the level of borrowings tends to be positively correlated with the *level* of money market rates irrespective of the level of the discount rate, because large borrowings arise only when banks are under pressure to contract their loans and investments and raise interest rates so as to protect their reserve positions. Ultimately, Riefler's explanation for fluctuations in market interest rates and the level of borrowings resides in an examination of factors supplying and absorbing reserves, and an attempt to distinguish between autonomous and induced changes in bank reserves.

A contrary interpretation, defending the borrowing for profit thesis, is expressed in R. Turner, *Member-Bank Borrowing* (Columbus: Ohio State University Press, 1938). The recent study by A. J. Meigs, *Free Reserves and the Money Supply* (Chicago: University of Chicago Press, 1962) effects a synthesis of these points of view.

The influence of member bank borrowing on excess reserve positions will depend in the final analysis on the Federal Reserve's administration of the discount window. If banks are permitted to borrow for profit without impairing their ability to borrow for purposes of meeting unexpected reserve deficiencies, and if such borrowing can be under-in the amount of this borrowing was thought to be the principal deterrent to precise Federal Reserve control over total member bank reserves, and hence, under constant desired reserve ratios, to precise Federal Reserve control over the volume of bank deposits and credit.

If the acceptance during the 1920's of the doctrine of stability in the cash ratios of commercial banks bordered on the uncritical, the subsequent disenchantment with this doctrine during the 1930's was perhaps equally extreme. In Britain the revelation by the Macmillan Committee's *Report*[9] of the extent to which the London clearing banks window-dressed their reported monthly cash positions by maneuvering their loans to the bill market contributed to the weakening of faith in the stability of cash ratios.

On the basis of his estimates of the true (i.e., un–window-dressed) "ratio" of cash to deposits for the London clearing banks, Richard Goodwin concluded: "The Ratio is by no means constant. From .112 in September 1921 it fell to .102 in May 1923 and to .090 by September 1931. From there it rose again to .109 in February 1934, and by October 1936 it had fallen to .090. Nor were these changes accidental or inexplicable; they were closely related to the major variations in banks' cash and the state of trade."[10] The burden of Goodwin's argument is to assert the dependence of the supply of money in part on the demand for loans, and the "impossibility of uniquely estimating even approximately the change in deposits which will be associated with any given change in reserves."[11]

Window-dressing is nowadays of much less significance than formerly, owing to the December, 1946, agreement of the banks to report their balance sheets on a common date each month and to aim for a true cash ratio of 8 per cent. In recent years the validity of basing monetary policy on constancy in the cash ratio has been questioned on rather different grounds. The Radcliffe Committee *Report* suggests that the Bank of England, in the interests of stabilizing the Treasury bill rate has created a

---

taken at a cost that is dependably below the cost of holding excess reserves to meet such deficiencies, then banks will have a strong incentive to hold negligible amounts of excess reserves. But if neither of these conditions are met, bank reluctance to borrow is likely to manifest itself in holding a somewhat larger amount of excess reserves than if such reluctance were absent.

[9] Great Britain, Committee on Finance and Industry, *Report* (London: His Majesty's Stationery Office, 1931), pp. 35–36, 156–57, 283–89, 302–3.

[10] R. M. Goodwin, "The Supply of Bank Money in England and Wales, 1920–1938," *Oxford Economic Papers*, V (June, 1941), 14. For a statistical analysis of the portfolio behavior of London banks, see A. J. Brown, "The Liquidity-Preference Schedules of London Clearing Banks," *Oxford Economic Papers*, I (October, 1938), 49–82.

[11] Goodwin, *loc. cit.*

situation in which Treasury bills are virtually the equivalent of cash, so that the cash ratio is no longer a factor limiting deposit creation.[12] Since the Bank of England, by its policies with respect to Treasury bills, has lost some of its control over bank cash, it has been suggested that a more realistic fulcrum for controlling the volume of bank deposits is the liquid assets ratio (the ratio of the sum of cash, money at call and short notice, and trade and Treasury bills to deposits). According to informal agreement among the clearing banks, when this ratio falls below 30 per cent, banks will tend to contract credit, and, conversely, when the ratio rises much above 30 per cent.[13] The Bank of England and the Treasury then jointly control the stock of high-powered money, defined to include Treasury bills as well as currency and bankers' deposits at the Bank of England.

In the United States, reaction against the notion that banks maintain a stable ratio of reserves to deposits turned to dismay as the volume of excess reserves mounted during the 1930's. At first, monetary policy was pictured as having an asymmetrical effectiveness:

Mr. Goldsborough: You mean you cannot push on a string.

Governor Eccles: That is a good way to put it, one cannot push on a string. We are in the depths of a depression and, as I have said several times before this committee, beyond creating an easy money situation through reduction of discount rates and through the creation of excess reserves, there is very little, if anything, that the reserve organization can do toward bringing about recovery. I believe that in a condition of great business activity that is developing to a point of credit inflation monetary action can very effectively curb undue expansion.

Mr. Brown: That is a case of pulling the string.

Governor Eccles: Yes. . . .[14]

As the decade wore on, and excess reserves continued to pile up, even the power to cause a contraction of the money supply seemed to be slipping away from the Federal Reserve:

In recent years, member bank reserve balances have grown so rapidly with the inflow of gold, and at the same time satisfactory loans and investments have been so limited, that banks have not followed the policy of investing all available funds. As a result banks hold tremendous amounts of excess reserves. . . .

[12] Great Britain, Committee on the Working of the Monetary System, *Report* (London: Her Majesty's Stationery Office, 1959), p. 128. The idea owes its origin to W. Manning-Dacey, *The British Banking Mechanism* (London: Hutchinson & Co., 1958), pp. 80–81.

[13] *Ibid.*

[14] U.S., Congress, House, Committee on Banking and Currency, *Hearings on H.R. 5357, Banking Act of 1935*, 74th Cong., 1st Sess., 1935, p. 377.

It is clear that at present reserve requirements do not act as an effective limitation on the expansion of bank credit and deposits. The real limitation is the availability of loans and investments satisfactory to banks. When, however, conditions again become favorable for an increase in bank loans and investments, there will be no effective means, under existing law, of exerting through reserves a restraining influence over a possible injurious credit expansion.[15]

The pendulum of opinion has swung back toward the position taken during the 1920's under the impact of the wartime and postwar return by banks to the holding of relatively small amounts of excess reserves in relation to deposits. Federal Reserve officials again[16] view the role of bank reserves in terms very reminiscent of the 1920's:

> The immediate focus of the Federal Reserve's policy instruments is such that the credit market partly gauges the direction of System monetary policy by observing closely the net position of banks—the difference between the aggregate of member bank reserves in excess of requirements and member bank borrowing at Reserve Banks. While the amount of reserves held in excess of requirements by member banks as a group will fall or rise to some extent with monetary restraint or ease, the movement of excess reserves is generally rather small. The volume of member bank borrowing, on the other hand, moves with greater amplitude in response to changes in monetary policy.[17]

The purpose of this study is to examine the validity of various hypotheses about factors determining the proportion of their assets that American banks hold in the form of excess cash reserves.

Chapter II presents a theory of bank profit maximization with special reference to factors determining the cash position that banks will desire to attain. The following two chapters examine the principal alternative hypotheses to explain the behavior of excess reserves of U.S. banks in the critical period of the 1930's when their accumulation led to a radical change in the interpretation put on them. Chapter V contrasts U.S. experience with the experience of Canada which met similar economic conditions in the 1930's, but with a very different banking structure. Chapter VI concentrates on the behavior of banks in New York City, in order to

[15] W. Thomas, "Monetary Controls," in *Banking Studies* (Washington: Board of Governors of the Federal Reserve System, 1941), pp. 341–42.

[16] During the past decade. In the war and early postwar period of pegged government securities prices, banks were able to treat their holdings of government securities as almost equivalent to cash. Consequently, their excess reserves were especially low in these years.

[17] R. A. Young, "Tools and Processes of Monetary Policy," in *United States Monetary Policy* (New York: American Assembly of Columbia University, December, 1958), p. 35.

extend the time horizon to include most of the period of the National Banking System that preceded the founding of the Federal Reserve System. This longer period contains several episodes that bear important similarities to the banking conditions prevailing during the 1930's. Chapter VII presents a number of statistical estimates of the liquidity preference functions of New York City banks before and after the founding of the Federal Reserve System. A final chapter of summary and conclusions is followed by several appendixes presenting additional detail on sources and methods used in the empirical phases of the study.

II

The Theory and Its Implementation

THIS CHAPTER presents the model of bank behavior to be tested in later chapters. It will be shown that a bank's demand for cash assets can be regarded as an application of the static theory of profit maximizing inventory policy under conditions of uncertainty.[1]

In the existing formal theory of banking,[2] the basic assumptions are: (a) banks maximize expected profits (or minimize expected losses),[3] (b) banks construct probability distributions of gains and losses from investment in assets, and (c) following the lead of Edgeworth,[4] profit maximization takes place subject to a specified distribution of cash drains during the planning period.[5]

The salient features of the static theory of banking can be illustrated by means of the following elementary model. Assume that a bank can hold two types of assets—non-interest bearing cash and fixed-interest bearing loans—and can issue three types of liabilities—non-interest bearing deposits repayable in cash on demand, short-term interest bearing debt, and equity securities. Suppose the bank attempts to minimize its expected losses during the planning period by appropriate allocation of its assets between cash and loans. Assume further that the return per

[1] K. Arrow, T. Harris, and J. Marschak, "Optimal Inventory Policy," *Econometrica*, XIX (1951), 250–72. A. Dvoretsky, J. Kiefer, and J. Wolfowitz, "The Inventory Problem: I. Cases of Known Distribution of Demand," *Econometrica*, XX (1952), 187–222.

[2] S. Karlin, "One Stage Inventory Models with Uncertainty," in K. Arrow, S. Karlin, and H. Scarf (eds.), *Studies in the Mathematical Theory of Inventory and Production* (Stanford, Calif.: Stanford University Press, 1958), pp. 109–34; R. C. Porter, "A Model of Bank Portfolio Selection," *Yale Economic Essays*, I (1961), 322–59; D. Orr and W. G. Mellon, "Stochastic Reserve Losses and Expansion of Bank Credit," *American Economic Review*, LI (September, 1961), 614–23.

[3] An expected utility maximization model of banking, assuming risk aversion, is presented in E. J. Kane and B. G. Malkiel, "Bank Portfolio Allocation, Deposit Variability and the Availability Doctrine," *Quarterly Journal of Economics*, LXXIX (1965), 113–34.

[4] F. Y. Edgeworth, "The Mathematical Theory of Banking," *Journal of the Royal Statistical Society*, LI (1888), 113–27.

[5] For a multiperiod programing model of bank portfolio behavior, see D. Chambers and A. Charnes, "Inter-temporal Analysis and Optimization of Bank Portfolios," *Management Science*, VII (July, 1961), 393–410.

dollar of loans over the planning period is composed of an interest component, y, known with certainty at the beginning of the period, and an expected capital gain or loss component, g, whose probability density is $\phi(g)$, where g is distributed over the range $-1 \leq g < \infty$. The bank is also faced with the prospect that there will be a cash drain or inflow. This expected change in cash will be expressed as a proportion, v, of initial deposits.[6] Let us suppose that the probability density of v is $f(v)$, where v is uniformly distributed over the interval $c \leq v \leq b$, and $c \geq -1$.[7] For simplicity, assume that the cash drain or inflow always occurs at the end of the period after all returns have been accrued on loans but before any of the loans are repaid. Finally, let us suppose that all cash deficiencies (i.e., all cash drains over and above the amount that can be covered by drawing down initial cash assets to zero) must be met by borrowing at short term or by sale of loans, and that the penalty per dollar of cash deficiency is n, a cost that is known with certainty at the beginning of the period. This penalty cost is equivalent to the interest rate on borrowed funds, or to the transactions cost on forced sale of loans, which might be interpreted as a brokerage fee or as the spread between the bid and the asked price on securities. The bank is assumed to operate in perfectly competitive markets so that y, n, and g are independent of the bank's own decisions.

Defining ρ to be cash as a ratio to initial deposits, the expected loss function $E[L(\rho)]$ can then be written as follows:

$$E[L(\rho)] = y\rho + \rho \int_{-1}^{\infty} g\phi(g)dg + \int_{c}^{-\rho} n(-v-\rho)f(v)dv, \quad (2.1)$$

where the first two terms taken together represent the expected alternative cost of holding cash instead of loans, and the third term represents the expected penalty cost of cash drains exceeding ρ. It is assumed that only \$1 of loans can be created by the individual bank, per dollar of excess reserves, because of a loss of all deposits created in the process of making loans. This is the simplest, but not necessarily the most descriptively accurate, assumption about the loan-deposit loss function.

[6] In this model it is taken for granted that all deposits created by lending are drawn down by the borrowers simultaneously with the granting of loans at the beginning of the period. Thus "initial deposits" refers to deposits remaining after loan-created deposits have been removed. Thus the model follows the usual textbook exposition of the deposit expansion multiplier process.

[7] Also note that we assume the bank is not subject to legal reserve requirements. A reserve requirement defined as a fraction, ρr, of deposits can be easily handled by redefinition of v as a cash drain or inflow over the interval $-1 + \rho r \leq c \leq v \leq b - \rho r$. The term "cash" then refers to bank reserves and vault currency in excess of legal reserve requirements.

Substituting $f(v) = 1/(b - c)$ in (2.1) and evaluating the integrals in the expression gives

$$E[L(\rho)] = y\rho + \bar{g}\rho - \frac{n\rho^2}{2(b-c)} + \frac{nc^2}{2(b-c)} + \frac{n\rho^2}{b-c} + \frac{n\rho c}{b-c}, \quad (2.2)$$

where $\bar{g}$ is the mean of g.

The first- and second-order conditions for a minimum are found by successive differentiation of (2.2) with respect to ρ.

$$\frac{\partial E}{\partial \rho} = y + \bar{g} + \frac{n\rho + nc}{b - c} \quad (2.3)$$

$$= 0 \text{ at a minimum or maximum}.$$

$$\frac{\partial^2 E}{\partial \rho^2} = \frac{n}{b - c} > 0, \text{ since } n > 0, \text{ by assumption.}$$

The demand for cash by the bank is derived from the minimized expression (2.3).

$$\rho = \frac{(c - b)(y + \bar{g})}{n} - c. \quad (2.4)$$

If we set $b = c + k$, where $k > 0$, (2.4) can be rewritten as

$$\rho = \frac{-k(y + \bar{g})}{n} - c. \quad (2.5)$$

Since the mean of the uniform distribution over the range $c \le v \le b$ is

$$\bar{v} = \int_c^b \frac{v}{b - c} \, dv = \frac{b + c}{2}, \text{ and } b = c + k, \text{ we have } \bar{v} = c + \frac{k}{2}.$$

Thus an expression for c in terms of $\bar{v}$ can be derived:

$$c = \bar{v} - \frac{k}{2}. \quad (2.6)$$

Substituting (2.6) in (2.5), yields a demand equation in terms of y, $\bar{g}$, n, $\bar{v}$, and k:

$$\rho = k\left[\frac{1}{2} - \frac{(y + \bar{g})}{n}\right] - \bar{v}.^8 \quad (2.7)$$

[8] If $k = 0$, $\rho = -\bar{v}$. But negative values of ρ are not possible in this simple model without reserve requirements. If there were reserve requirements and ρ were defined to be excess cash reserves, ρ could be negative. There arises the problem of defining a penalty for not meeting reserve requirements. We can neglect this complication in the simpler model.

Differentiating with respect to the parameters y, $\bar{g}$, n, $\bar{v}$, and k gives:

$$\frac{\partial \rho}{\partial y} = -\frac{k}{n} < 0 \qquad \frac{\partial \rho}{\partial \bar{v}} = -1 < 0 \qquad \frac{\partial \rho}{\partial \bar{g}} = -\frac{k}{n} < 0$$

$$\frac{\partial \rho}{\partial k} = \tfrac{1}{2} - \frac{(y + \bar{g})}{n} \qquad \frac{\partial \rho}{\partial n} = \frac{k(y + \bar{g})}{n^2} \geq 0 \, .^9$$

The demand for cash varies directly with the penalty cost of a cash deficiency and inversely with the interest rate on loans, the expected capital gain on loans, and the expected cash inflow. The sign of the change in cash with respect to a small increase in k, the range of the distribution of expected cash flows, cannot be determined without more precise knowledge of the values of y, $\bar{g}$, and n. The demand for cash varies directly with k if $n \geq 2(y + \bar{g})$, and inversely if $n < 2(y + \bar{g})$. This may appear to be a strange result, but its reasonableness can be shown on an intuitive level· Suppose, to begin with, that $k = 0$, so that the amount of cash drain, v, is certain to be equal to $\bar{v}$. In this event, the optimal cash ratio will be exactly equal to $-\bar{v}$. This much is clear from (2.7). Now suppose that we hold the expected cash drain, $\bar{v}$, constant while increasing k slightly. Should the bank hold a higher or lower cash ratio now that the exact amount of the cash drain, v, is not known with certainty? Surely the answer will depend on the costs of erring by holding a higher or lower cash ratio than the actual cash drain outcome would require. The unit cost of holding too much cash will be the foregone expected return on loans $(y + \bar{g})$. The unit cost of holding too little cash will be the penalty incurred in borrowing or forced liquidation of assets (n). The higher the expected return on loans relative to the penalty the more likely it is that an increase in k will encourage a bank to take a large risk of holding too little cash, by reducing its cash ratio below $-\bar{v}$. Conversely, if the return on loans is low relative to the penalty, an increase in k will lead the bank to avoid the risk of being short of cash by increasing its cash ratio. This ambiguity in the effect of a change in the dispersion of expected cash drains should therefore cause no surprise; it is a consequence of attempting to minimize expected losses by balancing the opposing earnings risks of having too much or too little cash.

It is important to bear in mind the various simplifications underlying this model of individual bank behavior, some of which have already been mentioned. Perhaps the most fundamental simplification lies in the ex-

---

[9] By assumption, $k > 0$ and $n > 0$, and if $(y + \bar{g}) > 0$, it follows that $\partial \rho / \partial n > 0$. Also it follows from (2.5) that $-\rho = c + k(y + \bar{g})/n \geq c$. If $-\rho < c$, the penalty effect on ρ is no longer operative since no penalty need be incurred. But only if $y + \bar{g} \leq 0$ would there be a reason for banks to hold cash in excess of any conceivable drain. It may be concluded that $\partial \rho / \partial n$ can never be negative.

tremely aggregative view that is taken of the bank's balance sheet. On the liability side the principal abstractions are that deposits and borrowings can be regarded as homogeneous entities, i.e., that distinctions between time deposits and demand deposits, or among personal, business, government, and interbank deposits, and distinctions between borrowings from the Federal Reserve and from other banks can all be neglected as being of secondary importance to the bank in making decisions as to the amount of cash it wishes to hold. If, for example, the expected cash drain or inflow depended on the proportion of time deposits to total deposits and the bank could control this proportion by varying the relative interest rates paid on time and demand deposits, the demand for cash would be a function of the proportion of time to total deposits and of the relative interest rates on demand and time deposits. Similarly, if there are several different kinds of penalty rates and if these penalty rates vary with the amount of funds to be acquired, the demand for cash will be a function of the several penalty rates.[10] In this study, however, the penalty rate will be interpreted typically to mean merely the discount rate on borrowing from the Federal Reserve, symbolized by d.

The model makes no pretense of being a full theory of bank asset portfolio behavior. Its sole objective is to provide a framework for the analysis of factors influencing the bank's demand for cash. In the context of the usual[11] fourfold division of bank assets into required reserves, primary reserves, secondary reserves, and risk assets, our focus is on primary reserves—those bank assets that can be converted into currency or deposits at essentially zero transactions costs. They include vault cash, excess reserves, and, possibly, deposits with other banks.[12] Lumping together these

[10] If there were more than one borrowing rate and if one of them were below the expected rate of return on loans, the bank would borrow an infinite amount of funds to make loans, quite apart from any need to meet cash deficiencies. The existence of finite borrowings must be attributable, in this model, to an excess of the penalty rate over the expected rate of return on loans. In this study my objective is to examine only the demand for cash and not borrowings.

[11] R. I. Robinson, *The Management of Bank Funds* (New York: McGraw-Hill Book Co., 1962), especially pp. 13–18. W. Steiner, E. Shapiro, and E. Solomon, *Money and Banking* (4th ed.; New York: Henry Holt & Co., 1958), pp. 123–52.

[12] Cash items in process of collection are not included in this concept of primary reserves on the grounds that, in the normal course of bank operations, an amount of deposits approximately equal to the total amount of cash items will be lost through the check clearing process, so that cash items in process do not ordinarily constitute a net addition to the available cash reserves of banks. We shall also want to subtract from deposits an amount equal to reported cash items as is done in calculating "net demand deposits subject to reserves." The Federal Reserve System's practice of granting "float" reserve credit to member banks on a schedule of "deferred availability" involves a concomitant reduction of cash items in process as reported by member banks and an increase in deposits subject to reserves.

three assets for the purpose of demand analysis can be justified if the alternative costs of holding these assets fluctuate in a strictly proportional manner[13] or if they are either perfect substitutes or perfect complements for each other. Probably the first of these grounds constitutes the best reason for treating these asset items as a unit, but it is recognized that none of the conditions is fulfilled except approximately. For the particular problems to be investigated in this study, it would not matter greatly if only excess reserves were considered to be cash, or if, on the other hand, the collection were broadened to include certain other highly liquid assets.

A more complete model might include demand and supply equations for each of the principal asset categories, and the demand for cash might be made a function of the expected return on each category of asset. An expanded model could throw light on such portfolio behavior problems as whether cash and risk assets[14] are substitutes or complements, as judged by cross elasticity of demand. Our model sidesteps these refinements by assuming that the earning assets of a bank can be viewed as a uniform class of assets under the general rubric "loans." The expected return on earning assets will be represented by the yield to maturity on short-term secondary reserve assets[15] denoted by the symbol r. It is assumed that the short-term yields to maturity are equal to the expected yields from holding longer-term secondary reserve assets for the same length of time, i.e., that short-term yields are unbiased estimates of expected yields on longer-term securities.[16] The only adjustment of this estimate of the yield on earning assets will be to allow for changes in the risk of loss from default of principal or interest on earning assets. If secondary reserve assets, from which the yield estimate is selected, were entirely free of variations in their default risk, this adjustment would be unnecessary, since in our model the return on secondary reserve assets can be assumed always to equal the expected return on other earning assets. Variations in the default risk of the entire spectrum of earning assets including secondary

[13] H. Wold and L. Jureen, *Demand Analysis* (New York: Wiley & Sons, 1953), pp. 108–9.

[14] Risk assets either lack marketability (i.e., have a high cost of quick conversion into cash) or have a relatively high risk of default. The two characteristics frequently go together.

[15] "Secondary reserves" include assets with low but non-zero transactions costs of quick conversion into cash, and which have only a moderate degree of uncertainty as to the amount that will be realized from their sale.

[16] This assumption has been the subject of much dispute. See D. Meiselman, *The Term Structure of Interest Rates* (Englewood Cliffs, N.J.: Prentice-Hall, Inc., 1962), and R. Kessel, "The Cyclical Behavior of the Term Structure of Interest Rates," Occasional Paper No. 91, National Bureau of Economic Research, 1965.

reserves is a different matter, however, and must be controlled statistically. This will be done by introducing the market yield spread between corporate bonds of different grade symbolized by P, as a variable in the statistical demand equation.

The tradition that incorporates the cash ratio of banks among the factors determining the money supply (see Chapter I) also lends support to our concentration on the cash position of banks to the exclusion of other items in the bank's portfolio. As a rule, emphasis on the crucial importance of the money supply in influencing the expenditure decisions of the public carries with it, implicitly or explicitly, the notion that credit effects, and specifically, those changes in the structure of the non-cash assets of the banking system that are not accompanied by changes in the money supply, play a distinctly secondary role in the determination of expenditures. The only structural changes in bank portfolio composition that really matter are those that cause changes in deposits or the money supply, and since these changes will necessarily affect the cash ratio of banks, they can be taken care of in an analysis of the determinants of the cash ratio.

With respect to the stochastic properties of the model, the main simplification is the assumption that v, the cash drain or inflow, is uniformly distributed. The assumption is defended only as an expository device, and not as a hypothesis to be tested. It is not unlikely that different probability distributions would yield similar predictions, but this possibility will be neither demonstrated nor explored in this study.

An empirical question of greater interest is the nature of the factors influencing banks in forming their expectations about v, and more particularly, about $\bar{v}$, the mean value of the probability distribution of cash drains and inflows. The fundamental distinction is between those factors determining cash flows that may be regarded as subject to relatively close control by the individual bank and those that are regarded as exogenously determined. For example, it may be reasonable to suppose that the individual bank knows the proportion of "derivative" deposits[17] that will be removed from the bank in consequence of lending. In this event, the bank can control the cash drain arising from its loan operations if it can control the volume of its loans. Again, if the bank can control the planned

---

[17] C. A. Phillips, *Bank Credit* (New York: Macmillan & Co., 1920), p. 40, differentiates between a primary deposit (". . . one that arises from the actual lodgement in a bank of cash or its readily convertible equivalent . . .") and a derivative deposit (". . . one which arises directly from a loan or which is accumulated by a borrower in anticipation of repayment of a loan"). In our model, primary deposits are the same as "initial deposits" owing to our special assumption about the relation between loans and derivative deposits.

volume if its outstanding borrowings, no uncertainty with respect to cash flows will arise from this source.[18] The same is true of equity capital.

Under these conditions, the main sources of uncontrolled disturbance to the bank's cash position would be uncontrolled variations in the volume of "primary" deposits.[19] Whatever the source of these uncontrolled variations, a basic hypothesis of this study is that the individual bank at any moment of time has a subjective probability distribution of expected cash inflows or drains during some subsequent interval and that $\bar{v}$, the mean of this probability distribution, tends to be high when the current level of cash is low relative to the amount the bank expects to possess on a permanent basis and conversely. One common-sense illustration of this is as follows: suppose the bank has experienced a recent sharp inflow of primary deposits that has raised total cash above the level the bank expects to maintain over the long run. Then the bank will expect a larger cash drain (or a smaller cash inflow) to occur in the near future than it would have expected in the absence of the inflow, i.e., the bank will expect a relatively low value of $\bar{v}$. Consequently, by our earlier argument, the bank would plan to hold a higher cash ratio than heretofore as a precaution against the increased likelihood of a cash drain.

It is apparent that the testing of this hypothesis about how expectations of cash drains are formed hinges on a specification of the process by which banks form their estimates of the permanent level of cash. This will be taken up in Chapter VII. A few preliminary comments on the nature of permanent cash are in order, however. First, our statistical tests will use observations on selected *groups* of banks or on all member banks of the Federal Reserve System. The assumption that total cash for the banking system is autonomously determined is undoubtedly more nearly valid than that an individual bank's cash is autonomously determined. Nevertheless, the ability of banks to borrow from the Federal Reserve and to set

[18] In our model, the planned level of borrowings is always zero, but this assumption can be modified.

[19] These distinctions between types of controlled and uncontrolled disturbances of the cash position are, of course, extreme. Preservation of "good will" often dictates that a bank permit its borrowers to exercise some control over the volume of its loans. And the volume of primary deposits, far from being exogenously determined, might be regarded as one of the bank's inputs which it seeks to acquire in optimal amounts, i.e., in competitive markets, up to the point where factor cost equals the value of marginal product. Unexpected divergences, however, between the market price for primary deposits and the price offered by the bank would lead to unexpected and possibly very wide fluctuations in its primary deposits. Therefore, even though the banker may attempt to adjust his service charges or rates of interest on time and demand deposits, occasions are likely to arise when his attempts are to some degree unsuccessful and he experiences a cash drain or a cash inflow.

the alternative cost to the public of holding currency versus deposits, enables banks to exercise some control over the nominal volume of their reserves.[20] But short-run variations in the cash reserves of the banking system may be regarded as largely beyond the control of banks as a group.

Second, in a banking system in which legal reserve requirements can be altered, or where differential reserve requirements exist among different classes of banks or types of deposits, changes in the average required reserve ratio, ρ_r, for a group of banks may exert disturbing influences on the group's cash in excess of legal requirements, quite apart from changes in the total volume of cash (including required cash reserves). The importance of the Federal Reserve in determining both total cash reserves and the average level of reserve requirements is overwhelming (in the short run, at least) and there is a high degree of interdependence between the two, as a consequence of conscious Federal Reserve policy. In view of this mutual determinacy, it would be reasonable for banks to form joint expectations about the permanent level of reserve requirements and total reserves. A variable combining both total reserves and the average reserve ratio in a manner appropriate to a policy by the monetary authorities of controlling the maximum deposit creation power of the banking system is R/ρ_r, where R denotes total reserves and ρ_r is the average required reserve ratio for the banking system, or for a selected group of banks. This variable is dubbed "potential deposits"; the difference between current potential deposits and permanent potential deposits will be designated "transitory potential deposits," symbolized by q. The specific hypothesis to be tested is that ρ varies *directly* with transitory potential deposits, q. In other words, q is the empirical counterpart of the theoretical construct $\bar{v}$. Whenever q is large, $\bar{v}$ is small, and conversely. In other words, if transitory potential deposits are high, this implies that banks anticipate an imminent large decline in cash, so that $\bar{v}$ would be small.

The variable k, representing the expected dispersion of the distribution of cash drains or inflows, will enter into the empirical work of later chapters in only a very minor way. In Chapter IV, a test of the effect of deposit instability on the demand for cash is presented, with inconclusive results. No other attempt is made to give empirical content to k. Nor is

---

[20] Of course, in the process of determining their desired ratio of cash to deposits, banks exercise control over their total reserves (for a given total of high-powered money and a given currency-deposit ratio). But this is not likely to be a significant qualification to our analysis in a banking system composed of more than a handful of independent units.

there much reason to suppose, from our model, that a clear test of its effect can be devised with the materials at hand.

Still another simplification is that the rate of turnover of deposits has no place in the banking model set forth previously. This follows from the timelessness of the model. All cash drains or inflows occur at one instant of time. A different approach, similar to the Tobin-Baumol models of the transactions demand for cash,[21] would handle cash drains as transactions of known unit size occurring with a known frequency per period of time. If transactions costs are positive, the amount of cash banks desire to hold might be expected to vary directly with the frequency of transactions, i.e., with the rate of deposit turnover. This proposition, however, is not tested in this study.

The demand for total cash will, of course, be greatly influenced by legal reserve requirements if these exist.[22] The first order effect of legal reserve requirements on the bank's total demand for cash can be eliminated from consideration by the expedient of defining the bank's balance sheet as net of required reserves—that is, by subtracting an amount equal to required reserves from both total cash and total deposits[23] This redefined deposit total will be designated "revised deposits."

[21] J. Tobin, "The Interest-Elasticity of Transactions Demand for Cash," *Review of Economics and Statistics*, XXXVIII (August, 1956), 241–47, and W. Baumol, "The Transactions Demand for Cash: An Inventory-Theoretic Approach," *Quarterly Journal of Economics*, LXVI (November, 1952), 545–56. Neither Tobin nor Baumol extend their analyses to take uncertainty into account.

[22] One technicality of some importance in a banking system with legal reserve requirements is the stringency with which the reserve requirement is applied. At one extreme, national banks before the Federal Reserve System began operation were required to maintain reserves up to the full legal minimum at all times. The principal penalty for failure to meet reserve requirements was that no new loans could be made except by purchase of sight bills of exchange. The Federal Reserve has evolved a system based on allowing a bank to meet reserve requirements on the average for a "reserve computation period" (semimonthly for country banks before December 31, 1959; one week, ending with Wednesday for central reserve and reserve city banks). The penalty for failure to meet requirements is an interest charge at 2 per cent per annum above the discount rate. A 2 per cent deficiency of reserves incurred in one reserve period, however, can be made up in the following period without penalty. At the other extreme, Canadian chartered bank required reserves are determined each month based on deposits for selected preceding Wednesdays. Reserve requirements may be met on the average for the month and till money held on the selected Wednesdays counts as reserves.

[23] Assets and liabilities associated with national bank note circulation (note liabilities, the required lawful money redemption fund, and the required reserve of Treasury bonds bearing the circulation privilege) can be excluded from the balance sheet on essentially the same grounds. Such miscellaneous minor items as customer's liability on acceptances, bank real estate, income collected but not yet earned, and acceptances outstanding can also be thought of as netted against total capital accounts.

The model is also specialized insofar as there is no role assigned to bank size as an influence on the desired cash ratio. The relevance of such a variable may be seen if we start by writing a demand function for bank cash in the more general functional form:

$$R = F(r, d, P, q, D, O) , \qquad (2.8)$$

where

R = nominal amount of bank cash desired
D = nominal amount of revised deposits
O = an index of prices relevant to bank operations
  (clerical wage rates and the like)
r = yield to maturity on short-term secondary reserve assets
P = spread between yields on bonds of different grades
q = transitory potential deposits .

If R can be supposed to be homogeneous of degree one in D and O, i.e., if

$$\lambda R = F(r, d, P, q, \lambda D, \lambda O) ,$$

by letting $\lambda = 1/D$, we obtain

$$\rho = \frac{R}{D} = G\left(r, d, P, q, \frac{D}{O}\right). \qquad (2.9)$$

From the formal point of view, this demand function for cash is implied by a modern quantity theory framework for the demand for money per unit of permanent income or wealth.[24] Alternatively, it would be possible to set $\lambda = 1/O$ and express the demand for cash in real terms.[25] Inasmuch as this procedure departs both from the traditional banking theory emphasis on the cash ratio and from the profit maximization model presented earlier, it will not be pursued. Moreover, empirical fitting of a real cash balance demand function by banks is inexpedient owing to lack of any usable and relevant monthly indexes of prices extending over the eight decades we shall later investigate. The same is true a fortiori for D/O which in (2.9) may be interpreted as a bank size variable.

Therefore, any attempt to test this bank size variable will be aban-

---

[24] M. Friedman, "The Quantity Theory of Money—a Restatement," in M. Friedman (ed.), *Studies in the Quantity Theory of Money* (Chicago: University of Chicago Press, 1956), pp. 3–24. In Friedman's framework, q would be regarded as a taste or utility determining variable, while r, d, and P would represent asset yield variables affecting the cost of holding cash.

[25] This appears to be the choice made in J. Gurley and E. Shaw, *Money in a Theory of Finance* (Washington: Brookings Institution, 1960), p. 258.

doned at the outset, no matter how serious the consequences in terms of specification error. The basic functional relation to be fitted, may be viewed as an incomplete version either of the inventory profit maximization model or of the modern quantity theory as applied to bank demand for cash. It may be written as follows:

$$\rho = H(r, d, P, q) . \qquad (2.10)$$

The desired cash ratio of banks (ρ) is a function of the yield on secondary reserve assets (r), the Federal Reserve discount rate, the spread between yields on bonds of different grade (P), and last but not least, transitory deposit potential (q).

The approach outlined is purely static; time has not been introduced in a way that is essential to the analysis. One is free to interpret this model of banking as simply a bank management game in which the banker-player makes his investment decisions and receives his payoff instantaneously.[26]

One step toward a dynamic model of bank behavior is to introduce lags in adjustment of the bank's expectations with regard to the permanent values assigned to variables affecting its demand for cash. Later we shall do just this in connection with developing a measurement of transitory deposit potential. But there is another type of lag, namely, lag in the adjustment of actual to desired cash positions. The two lags are conceptually different but troublesome to distinguish statistically in models involving both lags. Provided that a separation can be effected empirically, the introduction of lags in response of actual to desired cash involves the introduction of a new variable into the demand equation—the rate of change in cash, symbolized by $\dot{\rho}$. The equation becomes

$$\rho = M(r, d, P, q, \dot{\rho}) . \qquad (2.11)$$

[26] Edgeworth, *loc. cit.*, did, in fact, think of banking as a game of chance. Edgeworth's approach differs from the treatment presented here in that he conceived of a game in which a "disaster" (or bankruptcy) element was also involved. Setting a penalty value on this "disaster," the banker proceeds to minimize his losses or maximize his gains. Apparently Edgeworth was not optimistic about the possibilities for finding precise optimal solutions to the banker's portfolio problem and, instead, proposed to investigate the portfolio behavior of banks by "operational gaming," which nowadays goes under the name "simulation." If one were prepared to assign a penalty cost to bank failure as well as a criterion for the point at which failure occurs, the disaster problem could be integrated into our model, at least in principle. Finding appropriate empirical counterparts for these concepts is not likely to prove an easy task and is not attempted here. The penalty on forced liquidation of assets is not quite the same thing as a bankruptcy penalty. In still another respect, then, our model is rather specialized.

An alternative technique for handling disaster, based on choosing the course of action that would produce maximum gain for a given probability of disaster has come to be known as "safety first." See A. D. Roy, "Safety First and the Holding of Assets," *Econometrica*, XX (July, 1952), 431–49, and L. Telser, "Safety First and Hedging," *Review of Economic Studies*, XXIII (October, 1955), 1–16.

The empirical results presented in Appendix D do not suggest that $\hat{\rho}$ is a useful addition to the model. Therefore, to avoid misunderstanding of its relative importance in the study, further discussion of the disequilibrium variant of our model of stock demand for bank cash is relegated to Appendix A.

One final disclaimer is in order. In this study the aggregation question will, for the most part, be swept under the rug. To be sure, inasmuch as the principal empirical effort is directed at data for New York banks, one might hope for considerable similarity among individual bank elasticities or marginal propensities. But even so, the aggregation procedure does not satisfy the requirements for minimal aggregation bias,[27] so that such bias, with unknown characteristics, is undoubtedly present in our results.

[27] H. Theil, *Linear Aggregation of Economic Relations* (Amsterdam: North-Holland Publishing Co., 1954); R. G. D. Allen, *Mathematical Economics* (2d ed.; London: Macmillan & Co., 1960), p. 700.

III

Banking Experience in the United States during the 1930's: The Liquidity Trap Hypothesis

THE U.S. banking situation in the 1930–40 decade illustrates many of the empirical problems that will be encountered in applying the theoretical framework of the preceding chapter. The experience of the 1930's has been extremely important in affecting ideas about bank asset preferences. It led to widespread rejection of the notion that banks tend to maintain a stable ratio of cash to deposits and, hence, of the hope that the monetary authority can control the volume of deposit money by controlling the volume of bank reserves.[1] For these reasons, U.S. banking developments in this decade deserve to be reviewed.

EXCESS RESERVES DURING THE 1930's

The year 1931 marks a transition period in the long business decline of 1929–33. From 1929 to the middle of 1931, banks were subject to the usual strains of a severe business contraction. Total deposits of member banks fell 5 per cent and loans by almost 17 per cent between December 31, 1929, and June 30, 1931.[2] Investments increased, but by less than the loan decline. Total member bank reserves plus vault cash fell slightly, excess reserves increased somewhat, while borrowings from the Federal Reserve were paid off.[3] The decline in interest rates, while severe at the short-term end, was not unprecedented in U.S. money market experience.

Toward the end of 1930, the complexion of the depression began to change for the worse. Deposit liabilities of newly failed banks increased sharply in late 1930, subsided, and then rose again in June, 1931.[4] Starting

---

[1] In this study, I shall not examine the other side of the coin: those aspects of our monetary experience during the 1930's that engendered disillusionment about the effectiveness of controlling total expenditures by controlling the stock of money.

[2] U.S., Board of Governors of the Federal Reserve System, *Banking and Monetary Statistics* (Washington: Board of Governors, 1943), pp. 72–75.

[3] *Ibid.*, pp. 72–74, 397.

[4] *Federal Reserve Bulletin*, XXIII (September, 1937), 909.

in the spring of 1931 there was an accelerated decline in deposits and reserves, as bank failures continued in unprecedented numbers, and the public rushed to convert deposits into currency. In September, 1931, after England followed other European countries in suspending gold convertibility, an external gold drain intensified the panicky conditions that saw currency outside banks rise by 22 per cent between June 30 and December 31, 1931.[5] The recent Friedman and Schwartz study suggests 1931 to be the year in which a severe business slump turned into an economic catastrophe.[6]

For the remainder of the period up to the bank holiday, the distressed banking system sought any means available to build up the reserves needed to meet withdrawals of depositors. Loans were liquidated, and when deposit drains were heaviest, banks resorted to borrowing from the Federal Reserve. Excess and secondary reserves were also built up whenever and wherever feasible. The decline in short-term interest rates was abruptly halted in October, 1931, when the Federal Reserve Bank of New York's discount rate was raised from 1.5 per cent to 3.5 per cent in order to stem the drain of cash and gold. Then in February and June, 1932, the discount rate was lowered to 2.5 per cent, and between March and August, 1932, following passage of the Glass-Steagall Act, about $1 billion of U.S. securities were added to the Federal Reserve's account.[7] Short-term interest rates fell to extremely low levels as credit demands continued to slacken and banks sought to add to their holdings of secondary reserve assets. For the rest of the period, the Federal Reserve followed a largely passive monetary policy of allowing banks to borrow at 2.5 per cent interest—if they chose to, when even commercial paper rates were below 2.5 per cent—until shortly before the bank holiday of March, 1933, when the New York discount rate was again raised to 3.5 per cent. Between December 31, 1929, and March, 1933, some 8,942 banks closed their doors, three-fourths of them between June, 1931, and March, 1933.

Although there is little dispute that the actions of banks in the year and one-half before the bank holiday were mainly dictated by the desire to acquire cash and other liquid assets so as to protect themselves against depositor demands for cash, the behavior of banks for the remainder of the 1930's following the bank holiday has not been accorded such an unambiguous interpretation. Beginning in March, 1933, after most surviving

[5] *Banking and Monetary Statistics*, p. 34.

[6] M. Friedman and A. Schwartz, *A Monetary History of the United States, 1867–1960* (Princeton, N.J.: Princeton University Press for the National Bureau of Economic Research, 1963), pp. 299–419.

[7] *Banking and Monetary Statistics*, p. 371.

banks were reopened, business recovered rapidly, though not without a setback in 1934. Although member bank reserves, deposits, and total earning assets began to increase shortly after March, 1933, loans continued to be liquidated into the autumn of 1935.[8] During this recovery, banks more than doubled their holdings of government securities and member bank excess reserves increased from 2.0 per cent of net deposits subject to reserve in June, 1933, to 7.8 per cent in June, 1936.[9] Because large excess reserves were thought to pose a threat of "injurious credit expansion,"[10] the Federal Reserve, in successive increases between August, 1936, and May, 1937, doubled all reserve requirements, raising them to the legal maximum.[11] Excess reserves were cut drastically, from $2.9 billion in July, 1936, to $750 million in August, 1937. As part of the effort to prevent "excessive" stock market credit expansion, the Federal Reserve, prior to these moves, had raised margin requirements on stock exchange transactions.[12] More important, the Treasury, in December, 1936, reinforced Federal Reserve policies by initiating a gold sterilization program designed to stop the expansion of reserves arising from the gold inflow.[13] Instead of permitting gold to have an impact on bank reserves, the Treasury offset increases in reserves arising from gold inflows by purchasing the gold out of its balance at the Federal Reserve, replenishing these balances through sale of securities to the banks and the public rather than by issuance of gold certificates.

After the last increase in reserve requirements, bank loans at weekly reporting member banks continued to rise until mid-September, 1937, although investments began to be liquidated just before the first increase in requirements.[14] Deposits of weekly reporting banks began to decline in

[8] *Ibid.*, pp. 74–75.   [9] *Ibid.*, pp. 75, 396.

[10] U.S., Board of Governors of the Federal Reserve System, *Twenty third Annual Report* (Washington: Board of Governors, 1937), p. 216.

[11] The steps were as follows, starting from requirements on August 15, 1936:

	Aug. 15, 1936	Aug. 16, 1936	March 1, 1937	May 1, 1937
On Demand Deposits				
Central Reserve City Banks	13%	19.5%	22.75%	26%
Reserve City Banks	10	15	17.5	20
Country Banks	7	10.5	12.25	14
On Time Deposits	3	4.5	5.25	6

[12] *Ibid.*, p. 60.

[13] *Federal Reserve Bulletin*, XXIII (January, 1937), 1.

[14] *Ibid.*, pp. 152, 154. The increase was announced after the July 14, 1936, meeting of the Board of Governors and took effect one month later. Member banks therefore could have sold investments in anticipation of the increase.

the spring of 1937, while total loans and investments turned down shortly after the beginning of 1937.[15] Although the Board was convinced that its action in raising reserve requirements would not affect "easy money conditions now prevailing,"[16] yields on Treasury bills, notes, and bonds were all rising by the end of March, 1937, as were corporate and municipal bond yields. A bond price index based on yields for long-term U.S. government bonds fell from a peak of 103.8 in February, 1937, to a low of 99.4 in the first week of May.[17]

Beginning in August, 1937, and continuing throughout the rest of the 1930's, banks accumulated excess reserves to the unprecedented total of $6.8 billion in January, 1941. In that month, excess reserves of all member banks averaged 14.3 per cent of deposits subject to reserve.[18] Expansion in excess reserves was aided by release of $300 million of sterilized gold in September, 1937, by reduction of reserve requirements[19] on April 16, 1938, and by gradual desterilization over the next two years. In addition, the discount rate was lowered to 1 per cent, and the Federal Reserve, in September, 1939, engaged in its first significant open-market purchases of government securities since 1933. Total loans and investments of weekly reporting banks began to increase in August, 1938, investments having turned up in April. The trough in deposits was passed in June, while the turning point in loans was delayed until November.[20] Interest rates, after rising in the first nine months of 1937, descended to even lower levels than before—Treasury bill rates for the next three years hovered below one-tenth of 1 per cent, while yields on long-term governments declined to below $2\frac{1}{2}$ per cent.

The outstanding characteristic of bank asset structure in the aftermath of the bank holiday was, of course, the extremely high level to which excess reserves mounted. Several interpretations of this phenomenon have been offered. The explanation that gained the widest acceptance at the time was the one which provided the rationale for the Federal Reserve action of doubling reserve requirements in 1936–37.

[15] The series mentioned are seasonally unadjusted and typically have different cyclical turning points, even after seasonal adjustment. Loans, for example, frequently lag turning points in business activity while deposits tend to precede them. The National Bureau of Economic Research reference peak is May, 1937.

[16] *Twenty-third Annual Report*, p. 217.

[17] *Banking and Monetary Statistics*, pp. 460, 473.

[18] *Ibid.*, p. 396; *Federal Reserve Bulletin*, XXVII (March, 1941), 219.

[19] Reserve requirements for Central Reserve City banks' demand deposits were cut to $22\frac{3}{4}$ per cent, and roughly proportional reductions were made on requirements for other reserve categories.

[20] *Banking and Monetary Statistics*, pp. 156–57.

THE LIQUIDITY TRAP

The official Federal Reserve view of the large volume of excess bank reserves in 1936 was that they were redundant—an unintended result of the gold inflow:

These excess reserves have resulted almost entirely from the inflow of gold from abroad and not from the System's policy of encouraging full recovery through the creation and maintenance of easy money conditions. This easy money policy remains unchanged and will be continued.

The part of the excess reserves thus eliminated [by the increase in reserve requirements] is superfluous for all present and prospective needs of commerce, industry, and agriculture and can be absorbed at this time without affecting money rates and without restrictive influence upon member banks, practically all of which now have far more than sufficient reserves and balances with other banks to meet the increase.[21]

That the Federal Reserve authorities regarded themselves as powerless to induce banks to create more money is clearly indicated in statements made by Governor Marriner Eccles in hearings on the Banking Act of 1935:

Mr. Farley: In your speech at Columbus, you stated there were $24 billion in circulation. Do you think it would be a good thing if we increased that circulation?

Governor Eccles: How is it possible to increase it?

Mr. Farley: Why do we not use the authority we gave the executive department to issue $3 billion, to take up some of these bonds bearing interest?

Governor Eccles: How would that increase circulation?

Mr. Farley: Well, it would give these banks the actual cash instead of bonds.

Governor Eccles: What would they do with the cash? They would immediately send it back to the Federal Reserve bank and it would be in the Reserve banks as their excess reserves, and actual circulation would not change. The banks would have, in lieu of government bonds, $3 billion additional excess reserves.

Mr. Cross: Why not pay off all of the government bonds and get rid of paying any interest—because that would be inflation itself?

Governor Eccles: Here is what would happen: . . . such action would simply increase the reserves of the banking system by the amount of government bonds which were purchased with currency. The currency would go out, if it was $10 billion or $20 billion or $3 billion, whatever amount the government paid out in currency to retire its bonds; but the currency would immediately go into the banks and from the banks into the Federal Reserve banks . . . and you would just have additional reserves, additional excess reserves.[22]

[21] *Twenty-third Annual Report*, p. 216.

[22] U.S., Congress, House, Committee on Banking and Currency, *Hearings on H.R. 5357, Banking Act of 1935*, 74th Cong., 1st Sess., 1935, p. 321.

The opinion that the demand for credit controlled the extent to which bank reserves were utilized was succinctly expressed by J. W. Angell:

In a time of inactive demand for bank credit, with an enormous surplus of commercial bank reserves already being idle, it would not matter whether three billions [of federal government and related securities] or thirty were purchased [by the Federal Reserve Banks]. The immediate effect on business would be zero. And such has actually been the result to date. But if business and the demand for credit revive, then these open market operations, if carried out, will provide a very real and very dangerous foundation for a severe credit inflation— again at the wrong time.[23]

Angell was not alone in holding the position that under conditions of demand for credit existing in the post–bank holiday period, excess reserves of banks were truly idle funds performing no economic function. Other economists who expressed essentially the same view include Charles Hardy,[24] R. G. Hawtrey,[25] Benjamin Beckhart,[26] J. A. Schumpeter,[27] and the list could be extended. Many bankers also insisted that excess reserves were not needed—that all loan demands that gave promise of repayment were being met and could continue to be met if excess reserves were reduced. Perhaps the leader of this school of thought during the 1930's was Winthrop Aldrich of the Chase National Bank,[28] and this view was apparently accepted by the National City Bank,[29] the American Bankers Association,[30] and the Association of Reserve City Bankers.[31] Opinion was

[23] J. W. Angell, "Gold, Banks, and the New Deal," *Political Science Quarterly*, XLIX (December, 1934), 495–96.

[24] C. O. Hardy, "An Appraisal of the Factors ('Natural' and 'Artificial') which Stopped Short the Recovery Development in the United States," *American Economic Review, Papers and Proceedings*, XXIX (March, 1939), 170–82.

[25] R. G. Hawtrey, "The Credit Deadlock," in A. D. Gayer (ed.), *The Lessons of Monetary Experience* (New York: Farrar & Rinehart, 1937), pp. 130–44.

[26] B. Beckhart, "Domestic Aspects of Credit Control and the Recovery Program— Discussion," *Proceedings of the Academy of Political Science*, XVII (1936–38), 32.

[27] J. A. Schumpeter, *Business Cycles* (New York: McGraw-Hill Book Co., 1939), II, 1019–30.

[28] W. W. Aldrich, "Credit Control under a Recovery Program," *Proceedings of the Academy of Political Science*, XVII (1936–38), 27.

[29] As reported in K. D. Roose, *The Economics of Recession and Revival* (New Haven, Conn.: Yale University Press, 1954), p. 100.

[30] Research Council, American Bankers Association, *The Answers of the American Bankers Association in Reply to Part 9 of the Questionnaire of the Committee on Banking and Currency of the United States Senate* (New York: The Association, 1941), p. 123.

[31] J. H. Riddle, "The Problem of Excess Reserves, Report Prepared for the Commission on Banking Law and Practice of the Association of Reserve City Bankers, January 1936" (Chicago: The Association, 1936) pp. 1–11. Also see *The Answer of the Association of Reserve City Bankers to the Questionnaire on National Monetary and Banking Policy Issued by the Committee on Banking and Currency, United States Senate* (Chicago: The Association, 1941), p. 91.

not unanimous, of course, even among New York bankers. Leffingwell of J. P. Morgan and Company, put himself on record as opposed to the Aldrich position.[32] But on the whole, bankers represented themselves as eager to make loans and denied allegations of ultra-conservatism in their credit policies. An official of the American Bankers Association testified in 1939 that "thousands of banks" were running advertisements offering to loan money.[33]

The argument that banks were surfeited with excess reserves for lack of sufficient credit demand to utilize them implies that bank behavior in the late 1930's exemplified an "absolute" preference for liquidity in the Keynesian sense.[34]

In its simplest form this doctrine, which is also known as the "liquidity trap," states that the demand schedule for cash as a function of the interest rate will become infinitely elastic at some low but positive interest rate. A corollary, in the case of banks, is that at low interest rates on bank assets the demand by the banks for loans and investments will become infinitely elastic. At such a low level of interest rates, banks will be entirely indifferent to the relative amounts of excess reserves and loans and investments that they hold. The volume of excess reserves will be determined completely by the amount of total reserves and by the volume of borrowing from banks that the public and the government undertake at given interest rates. Therefore a monetary policy designed to increase the volume of *total bank credit* through open-market purchases of government securities would be self-defeating.[35] Banks would simply hold more excess reserves and less loans and investments.[36]

[32] R. Leffingwell, "Economic Recovery and Monetary Stabilization Introductory Remarks," *Proceedings of the Academy of Political Science*, XVII (1936–38), 100.

[33] A typical advertisement, by the First National Bank and Trust Company, Minneapolis, asked: "Here is the money, but where are the borrowers?" See statement of Robert M. Hanes, first vice-president of the American Bankers Association and president of the Wachovia Bank and Trust Company, Winston-Salem, North Carolina, in U.S., Congress, Senate, Subcommittee of the Committee on Banking and Currency, *Hearings on S. 1482 and S. 2343, To Provide for Insurance of Loans to Business*, 76th Cong., 1st Sess., 1939, p. 157.

[34] J. M. Keynes, *The General Theory of Employment, Interest and Money* (New York: Harcourt, Brace & Co., 1936), p. 207.

[35] Purchase of bonds entirely from the banks would reduce the total amount of bank credit; at unchanged interest rates, there is no reason to suppose the public will offer to sell bonds to the banks to replace the bonds that banks have sold to the central bank. But it does not follow that monetary policy designed simply to expand the volume of money would be thwarted, since purchase of bonds from the public would automatically increase currency and/or bank deposits, quite apart from whether or not banks held idle any resulting increment to their excess reserves.

[36] A thoroughly consistent monetary policy of increasing the volume of total bank credit would, under these circumstances, require, paradoxically, the *selling* of govern-

This is the liquidity trap concept that seems implicit in the position of Governor Eccles and the Board of Governors of the Federal Reserve System as quoted earlier; support for such a viewpoint might be derived from Figure 1, Panel A, which depicts the excess reserve ratio of all member banks as a function of short-term interest rates. The figure shows a tendency for the apparent demand schedules for excess reserves to become perfectly flat at low short-term interest rates.[37]

If this scatter is taken as an accurate representation of the demand curve for excess reserves, the desire of the Board of Governors, during the middle and late 1930's, to re-establish control over the reserve position of member banks would seem to call for increases in reserve requirements sufficient to move banks back to the "corner" of their demand schedule—the place where the demand curve's slope changes most rapidly.[38] At the corner, increases or decreases in the volume of bank reserves would cause shifts in the banks' willingness to create deposits and loans and investments. But, even so, open-market purchases must proceed with caution after the corner position is reached; otherwise, monetary control would be back where it started before the increase in reserve requirements. The Board's actions in the spring and autumn of 1937, when it purchased rather small amounts of government bonds, might seem to be consistent with this theory.[39]

Of course, the liquidity trap hypothesis is an ex post formalization of the views that led up to the 1936–37 reserve requirement changes. Few economists, and still fewer bankers and government officials, expressed themselves in a Keynesian framework at the time. Indeed, one of the earliest American Keynesians felt the Federal Reserve went too far in 1936–37. In 1942, Samuelson criticized the doubling of reserve requirements.

It is more and more being realized that reserves do *not* perform the function of till money. Rather they are felt to be necessary for maximization of income over

---

ment bonds to banks by the central bank. Of course, advocates of the credit approach to monetary policy typically direct their attention to particular types of credit such as business loans.

[37] If the excess reserve ratio is plotted against the logarithm of the short-term interest rate, this tendency is by no means evident. See Figure 6, where such a plotting is made for New York City banks' excess cash reserve position.

[38] J. H. Kareken, "Our Knowledge of Monetary Policy," *American Economic Review, Papers and Proceedings*, LI (May, 1961), 42.

[39] U.S., Board of Governors of the Federal Reserve System, *Twenty-fourth Annual Report* (Washington: Board of Governors, 1938), pp. 6, 10.

time in a world where uncertainty dictates diversification of portfolios. This the Reserve authorities overlooked when they raised reserve requirements in 1936–37. They were unprepared for the resulting pressure on the market for governments, since they regarded excess reserves as surpluses. Actually, the banks tried to reestablish old excess reserve ratios.[40]

Samuelson clearly was of the opinion that banks were not in a liquidity trap position in 1936–37. According to his interpretation, the interest rate floor was gradually declining.

First, there has been a gradual downward shift in the banks' liquidity preference schedules in recent years. Over time they would be willing to hold more and more governments and less and less cash at the same rates of interest in consequences of their fading recollection of high rates. (Our observations of growing excess reserves are not inconsistent with the above statement, if careful distinction is made between shifts of a schedule and movements along the schedule.) Second, the liquidity preference schedules of both banks and the public have been so elastic as to create a broad margin of indifference between the holding of money substitutes and money (deposits for individuals, Federal Reserve deposits for banks). Consequently, induced changes in the interest rate are negligible.[41]

In other words, at any given point in time, a liquidity trap exists, but as the current long-term rate of interest declines, expectations of future long-term rates of interest are revised downward. This causes the liquidity preference schedule to shift downward and to the left. In the process of shifting, banks absorb more bonds, but at the same time, an increase in bank reserves will tend to cause a movement *along* the liquidity preference curve defined as a function of the long-term interest rate.

In this formulation of the liquidity trap, it is not correct to claim that a monetary policy of increasing bank reserves through open-market operations would be ineffective. It would seem that in order for expected long rates to *continue* to be revised downward, the actual long rate must continue to decline. Open-market operations, could serve the purpose of maintaining downward pressure on the current long-term rate of interest.

[40] P. A. Samuelson, "Fiscal Policy and Income Determination," *Quarterly Journal of Economics*, LVI (August, 1942), 594. Criticisms of a similar nature were made in A. H. Hansen, *Full Recovery or Stagnation* (New York: W. W. Norton, 1938), pp. 286–87, and *Fiscal Policy and Business Cycles* (New York: W. W. Norton, 1941), pp. 79–82. Also see P. A. Samuelson, "Recent American Monetary Controversy," *Three Banks Review*, XXIX (March, 1956), 7.

[41] Samuelson, "Fiscal Policy and Income Determination," p. 595.

It matters very little for monetary policy whether a given reduction in interest rates is accomplished by a movement along a liquidity preference curve or by a combination of a downward shift of the curve and a movement along the curve, so long as both adjustments are attributable in the end to a central bank policy that permits rapid expansion of bank reserves.

Samuelson's hypothesis may be useful in explaining the behavior of excess reserves in the late 1930's and early 1940's. But it is not the basis for the "can't push on a string" doctrine. This doctrine regards banks as entirely passive with respect to their excess reserve position. In the liquidity trap, as so envisaged, changes in excess reserves are the consequence of factors beyond the control of banks, such as Federal Reserve policy on reserve requirements and open-market operations, and attitudes of the borrowing public with respect to their demand for bank credit. To be consistent with the string doctrine, the liquidity preference curve for banks must be perfectly elastic at some unchanging low level of interest rates.

Advocates of the string doctrine tended to view the supposed passivity of banks as almost axiomatic; little attention was devoted to justifying it as a theorem by reference to more basic economic forces. It is not difficult, however, to find support for the passivity hypothesis and its liquidity trap corollary, in the three Keynesian motives for holding money.

For example, during the later 1930's, banks may have become indifferent as between holding cash or Treasury bills because at some low but positive interest rate on bills the return from bill holdings, net of transactions costs, were zero.[42] Some crude versions of this transactions demand hypothesis imply that banks have no reason to diversify their asset holdings—holding only bills at rates higher than the critical interest rate and only cash at lower rates—but the more sophisticated versions of the transactions demand theory are free of this peculiarity.[43]

---

[42] That the critical interest rate could be extremely low is suggested by the fact that interest rates on new issues of Treasury bills in 1939 and 1940 were frequently less than one-hundredth of 1 per cent and were sometimes even negative. See *Banking and Monetary Statistics*, p. 460. The negative bill rates are deceptive as measures of the yield on Treasury bills: some states (Michigan, South Carolina, and North Carolina) impose property taxes on bank capital but allow government securities to be deducted from the tax base. Others, such as Illinois, impose a personal property tax on bank deposits that can be avoided by holding Treasury bills over the assessment date. See National Industrial Conference Board, *The Taxation of Banks* (New York: The Conference Board, 1934), pp. 25–27, and *Commercial and Financial Chronicle*, January 7, 1939, p. 11. The net return on Treasury bills to investors in these states was therefore not negative.

[43] See W. Baumol, "The Transactions Demand for Cash: An Inventory-Theoretic

While the transactions motive suggests a reason why there may be a liquidity trap with respect to rates on short-term liquid assets, the speculative motive provides a reason for a similar phenomenon with respect to long-term bond yields. Bankers in the 1930's may have expected long-term interest rates to rise by enough to wipe out, through capital losses, the income earned on bond investment at the currently prevailing levels of long-term interest rates. In a choice between holding cash and long-term bonds, bankers with these expectations would have chosen cash.

The simplest versions of the speculative motive suffer from the same critical defect as the crude versions of transactions demand—inability to explain diversification of bank portfolios between cash and other earning assets. Also the usual grounds for a speculative liquidity trap—less than unitary elasticity of expectations regarding bond interest rates—is open to the objection that it is a temporary phenomenon. Investors would eventually come to regard any level of the current bond rate as normal, if that rate persists long enough. To salvage the speculative model, it must be combined with some form of precautionary motive. This is the explicit objective of one such hybrid. It assigns to the precautionary motive the role of "giving the speculative motive something to bite on."[44] Interest rate uncertainty and risk aversion (desires for capital or income stability) are introduced to provide a motive for diversifying asset holdings.

A more frequently encountered formulation emphasizes that uncertainty of expected future prices is greater for bonds than for cash.[45] On the assumption that lenders are risk averters with respect to these expectations, but that borrowers are not, a liquidity premium will be reflected in the spread between the bond rate of interest and the pecuniary yield on cash. The existence of this liquidity premium establishes the *possibility* of a permanent long-run liquidity trap at a positive interest rate, i.e., at a positive spread between the pecuniary yields on bonds and money. There

---

Approach," *Quarterly Journal of Economics*, LXVI (November, 1952), 547, and J. Tobin, "The Interest-Elasticity of Transactions Demand for Cash," *Review of Economics and Statistics*, XXXVIII (August, 1956), 241–47.

[44] R. F. Kahn, "Some Notes on Liquidity Preference," *The Manchester School*, XXII (September, 1954), 246.

[45] J. R. Hicks, *Value and Capital* (Oxford: Oxford University Press, 1946), pp. 141–70. N. Kaldor, "Speculation and Economic Stability," *Review of Economic Studies*, VII (October, 1939), 1–27. Both Hicks and Kaldor develop Keynes's outline of the interaction between speculative and precautionary motives, as set forth in the *General Theory*, pp. 168–69, and in the *Treatise on Money*, II, 142–44.

are two factors that may alter this spread: changes in the liquidity premium and changes in mean expected future price of bonds. It is difficult, empirically, to separate these two influences on the demand for money because of the paucity of evidence on their independent effects.[46]

The search for a liquidity trap hypothesis based on a single Keynesian motive has also included reliance on the precautionary motive alone. A model has been devised in which the liquidity trap may arise entirely out of the precautionary motive evoked by risk aversion in the face of uncertainty with respect to the future course of interest rates.[47] The probability distribution of expected capital gains and losses from holding long bonds is assumed to have a zero mean and the investor is assumed to maximize the expected utility of income (including interest and capital gains or losses) from holding cash and bonds. The demand for money in this model is a function of the average interest rate on non-cash assets and the expected variance of the rate of capital gain or loss on these assets.

There is no need to confine ourselves to Keynesian formulations of the demand for cash. A liquidity trap is a possibility in the banking-inventory model of Chapter II. The elasticity of ρ with respect to y in (2.7) is $(-k/n)\,(y/\rho)$. This elasticity goes to infinity as either k, the range of expected cash inflows or outflows, goes to infinity or as n, the penalty on forced asset liquidation, goes to zero. If there is a negative net return on earning assets (i.e., if $y + \bar{g} < 0$), the bank would want to hold all its assets in cash even if y is positive. But this is not to be confused with a liquidity trap, that is, a condition of infinite elasticity of demand for cash.

In summary, it is clear that a wide variety of models are capable of generating a liquidity trap. They differ among themselves in the relative emphasis given to the short-term versus long-term interest rates and in the importance assigned to variables other than the interest rate—volume of transactions, expected cash drain, expected variance of bond prices, default risk, and liquidity premiums. No attempt will be made to find empirical counterparts for each of these variables. The primary effort of this study is not directed at confirmation or rejection of every conceivable variant of the liquidity trap hypothesis. Rather it is the exploration of alternative hypotheses to explain bank behavior, especially in the 1930's.

[46] This point comes up again in connection with the Friedman-Schwartz explanation of bank assets and yield spreads in the 1930's. See below, pp. 41–43, 51–52, 55–58.

[47] J. Tobin, "Liquidity Preference as Behavior toward Risk," *Review of Economic Studies*, XXV (February, 1958), 74–79. Also see H. Markowitz, *Portfolio Selection* (New York: John Wiley & Sons, 1959), and H. Theil, *Economic Forecasts and Policy* (Amsterdam: North-Holland Publishing Co., 1958), pp. 402–31.

Nevertheless, in testing the leading alternative explanation, it will be possible also to make some regression tests of the validity of the liquidity trap hypothesis.[48]

[48] Statistical fitting of linearized liquidity preference schedules to determine whether interest elasticities are actually infinite is futile. My procedure will be to run regressions of the excess reserve ratio on the short-term interest rate for different time periods, then compute and compare the *elasticities* of the fitted lines. If high elasticities are associated with periods in which interest rates tend to be low, then I shall accept this as evidence favoring, but not confirming, the liquidity trap hypothesis. This test procedure is similar to that of M. Bronfenbrenner and T. Mayer, "Liquidity Functions in the American Economy," *Econometrica*, XXVIII (1960), 810–34.

It has been suggested that the liquidity trap hypothesis would be confirmed by evidence that *slopes* of liquidity preference curves tend to be greater at low-interest rates. This position is unacceptable, if we understand "liquidity trap" to mean a horizontal money demand curve at a non-negative interest rate, and not simply that the *amount of cash demanded goes to infinity* at a non-negative interest rate. The latter interpretation does not carry with it the implication that monetary policy is impotent, which is ordinarily associated with the liquidity trap doctrine. A demand curve of constant elasticity, with steadily increasing *slope* at lower interest rates, satisfies the requirement that cash demanded goes to infinity as the interest rate approaches zero asymptotically. But such a demand curve never becomes horizontal; a minimum requirement for this is that the elasticity must increase progressively as the interest rate falls. Clearly the elasticity must attain infinity, not merely approach it, but owing to limitations of statistical estimation we must be satisfied with testing the approach. See the notes and comments of Professors R. Eisner, T. Mayer, M. Bronfenbrenner, and A. Meltzer in *Econometrica*, XXXI (July, 1963), 531–50.

IV

Alternative Explanations of Banking in the 1930's: Shifting of Liquidity Preferences

WHILE THE EXISTENCE of a liquidity trap has been the prevailing interpretation of the large volume of excess reserves held by banks during the middle and late 1930's, it is possible to assemble some conflicting opinions and evidence. There is one unifying thread to all of it: the view that banks held abnormal amounts of excess reserves, not because of their passivity or indifference, but because it was the prudent thing to do under the circumstances. The banking climate of the 1930's led banks to *want* to hold more "excess" cash for given interest rate levels than they ever wanted to hold before. In other words, their liquidity preference schedules shifted upward and to the right. Corresponding to this shift there was a reduced willingness of banks to extend credit, particularly for ordinary business purposes.

This chapter will examine some of the arguments and factual support for this position. In chapters to follow, other implications of the shift hypothesis will be explored, culminating in Chapter VII with extensive statistical time series investigation of New York City banks. In the first section of the present chapter several pieces of preliminary evidence bearing on the comparative validity of the liquidity trap and shift hypothesis will be summarized and evaluated. The second section will explore some of the factors that may have been responsible for the shift if in fact one did occur.

THE PRELIMINARY EVIDENCE

A. Borrower Interview Surveys

Evidence of banker reluctance to lend during the 1930's was gathered in a spate of questionnaire surveys of borrower experience in obtaining bank credit. The most famous and most diligent of these surveys (if the pains taken to uncover unsatisfied borrowers is any standard) was the one conducted in 1934 by Charles Hardy and Jacob Viner at the request of the U.S. Treasury Department.[1] Some 1,788 cases of loan refusals, oc-

---

[1] C. O. Hardy and J. Viner, *Report on the Availability of Bank Credit in the Seventh Federal Reserve District* (Washington: U.S. Government Printing Office, 1935).

curring between the bank holiday and September 1, 1934, in the Chicago Federal Reserve District were tabulated and analyzed. The findings were summarized as follows:

1. That there exists a genuine unsatisfied demand for credit on the part of solvent borrowers, many of whom could make economically sound use of working capital.

2. That the total amount of this unsatisfied demand for credit is considerably smaller than is popularly believed, but is large enough to be a significant factor, among many others, in retarding business recovery.

3. That a very large proportion of would-be borrowers are persons whose equity in the business they control is so small that any bank or individual who lends them substantial amounts is assuming a major part of the risk of the business, rather than the normal risk of a creditor.

4. That there is a larger unsatisfied demand for long-term working-capital credit than for one-turnover loans.

5. That one of the most serious aspects of this unsatisfied demand is the pressure for liquidation of old working-capital loans, even sound ones.

6. That this pressure is partly due to a determination on the part of bankers to avoid a recurrence of the errors to which they attribute much of the responsibility for the recent wave of bank failures.

7. That it is also due in large part to the attitude of bank examiners, both State and national.

8. That so far as small business is concerned, the difficulty in getting bank credit has increased more, as compared with a few years ago, than has the difficulty in getting trade credit.

9. That efforts to relieve this stringency through direct lending on the part of the Federal Reserve Bank of Chicago and the Chicago agency of the Reconstruction Finance Corporation have so far had a negligible effect on the general state of credit.[2]

In 1935, the U.S. Census Bureau released a survey conducted in the summer of 1934 of credit and capital experience of small manufacturers in 1933. It was found that 44.8 per cent of 4,387 manufacturing establishments reported to be borrowers had experienced difficulties in obtaining credit.[3] Percentages of concerns reporting difficulties varied inversely with size of establishment,[4] ratio of net worth to debt, and ratio of current assets to current liabilities. Even among establishments with equity-debt and "current" ratios of over 3.0, about 17.5 per cent experienced credit difficulties. As reported by Roos: "Derived from this same survey were criti-

[2] *Ibid.*, p. vi.

[3] Based on a summary of the Census Report in C. Roos, *NRA Economic Planning* (Bloomington, Ind.: Principia Press, 1937), pp. 388–94.

[4] The survey covered establishments with 20 to 125 employees.

cisms of the inadequacy of sources of credit from all classes of manufacturers, . . . the complainants, in general, charging that the mania of banks for liquidity, invited by bank examiners, had resulted in the restriction of loans."[5]

Since both the Census Bureau and the Hardy-Viner surveys refer to credit conditions in the months immediately following the bank holiday, they are not necessarily indicative of the availability of credit in later years of the 1930's, when excess reserves reached truly unusual levels. Evidence on borrower experience in these years was gathered in a National Industrial Conference Board survey (made for the American Bankers Association) of 1,755 assorted concerns, the bulk of them manufacturers who replied to a mail questionnaire in 1938.[6] According to the Conference Board: "The most important finding of the survey is that over 91 per cent of the concerns reported either no bank credit experience or no bank credit difficulty in recent years. Out of the 1,755 returns tabulated, 448, or 25.5 per cent, stated that they had not had any credit experience with banks, and 1,153 or 65.7 per cent reported that they had not had any difficulty in obtaining sufficient bank credit to meet their legitimate requirements."[7]

Thus about 11.8 per cent of firms seeking loans from banks reported either refusal or restriction of credit. But the Conference Board's sample includes 704 concerns employing over 100 people, whereas the upper cutoff point in the aforementioned Census survey was 125 employees.[8] Out of the 404 firms in the Conference Board survey, which employed less than 100 workers and which sought bank credit, 19.1 per cent reported difficulties.[9] This compares with 44.3 per cent for manufacturing concerns of roughly comparable size in the Census survey for 1933. Taken at face value, the Conference Board survey would indicate a considerable lessening of credit stringency in the period intervening between 1933 and 1938.[10]

[5] Roos, *op. cit.*, p. 392.

[6] L. H. Kimmel, *The Availability of Bank Credit, 1933–1938* (New York: National Industrial Conference Board, 1939), pp. 47–104. A similar survey made by the Conference Board in 1932, at the request of the Federal Reserve Bank of New York, falls outside the period with which we are presently concerned. See R. A. Young, *The Availability of Bank Credit* (New York: The Conference Board, 1932).

[7] Kimmel, *op. cit.*, pp. 52–53.

[8] Out of the 1,755 concerns, 528 were unclassifiable by number of employees. *Ibid.*, p. 68.

[9] *Ibid.*

[10] The period of borrower experience covered by the Conference Board survey is

To assess the degree of credit restriction these results imply, it is necessary to make a comparison with borrower experience in a "normal" period. In this connection, it is worth noting that a Department of Commerce survey of small business financing in the twelve-month period ended June 30, 1954, indicated that 46 per cent of the firms in the survey which sought "outside financing" (a broader concept than bank financing) were unable to obtain "all the funds they wanted."[11] While the Commerce survey covered mostly a recession period, it should be remembered that 1937–38 was also a period of depressed business activity.

In view of the contention of the supporters of the liquidity trap hypothesis that all "legitimate" credit demands were being met in the late 1930's, one would expect the proportion of disappointed borrowers to be less in the late 1930's than in more "normal" periods. Although a "fringe of unsatisfied borrowers" may always exist, that fringe should be smaller when the demand for loan assets by banks is infinitely elastic than when it is not. The evidence from the borrower surveys tends to support the idea that the loan demand function of banks was more elastic during the late 1930's than it was in either 1933 or 1953–54. But the underlying crudities of the survey procedures, and the ambiguities of interpretation that attend the few comparisons that can be made, make this a highly tentative conclusion.

B. Statistical Studies of Bank Reserves and Bank Credit

A different body of evidence on willingness of banks to extend credit during the 1930's has been examined in two studies, one by George

---

1933–38. The bulk of the cases of loan refusal or restriction, however, that could be classified by year of most recent refusal or restriction occurred in 1937 or 1938.

By covering a six-year period of borrower experience, it is possible the Conference Board survey imparted a downward bias to the proportion of loan refusals or restrictions relative to total concerns seeking bank credit. Borrowers who have recently had their loan requests turned down are more likely to respond to a mail questionnaire than those for which the experience is not so fresh, whereas for borrowers who have had no credit difficulties, this tendency to respond on the basis of recent experience is not so likely to be pronounced. The rate of response to the questionnaire (1,755 tabulated responses out of 9,000 mail inquiries) allows plenty of leeway for this factor to operate.

One may also question whether the joint auspicies of the National Industrial Conference Board and the American Bankers Association would be regarded by disappointed borrowers as a sympathetic or even impartial sounding board for their complaints on availability of credit.

[11] L. F. McHugh and J. N. Ciaccio, "External Financing of Small and Medium Size Business," *Survey of Current Business*, XXXV (October, 1955), 18. Ninety per cent of the concerns in the survey employed less than 50 people. Only 1 per cent employed more than 250 people.

Horwich,[12] the other by the late Edward Kilberg.[13] Horwich summarized his approach and results as follows:

> This study attempts to discover whether member bank earning assets were causally related to total reserves during the period 1929–39. Utilizing quarterly call-report data, total earning assets of member banks, E, were related to the system's "effective reserves," R''—a series in which nominal reserves are adjusted to incorporate all changes in the capacity to use reserves (e.g., a lowering of the reserve requirement is expressed as an increase in the quantity of effective reserves). The scatter diagram between E (on the vertical axis) and R'' (on the horizontal axis) failed to reveal a consistent relationship between the two variables. There was a strong positive correlation between R'' and E from June, 1933 to March, 1936, and again from June, 1938 to December, 1939. However, the regression line for the latter period had a substantially higher intercept than the line for the earlier period. The intervening points—those for March, 1936 to June, 1938, during which the Federal Reserve reduced effective reserves by doubling reserve requirements—fall (with considerable dispersion) along a horizontal line. Thus, in this intermediate interval, the aggregate holdings of earning assets by bankers were essentially unaffected by declining reserves. This suggests that in spite of high positive correlation between R'' and E in the periods indicated, R'' may not have exerted a causal influence on the level of earning assets. In fact, the series on earning assets coincides exactly with the National Bureau's turning points of business activity, and correlates impressively with a quarterly index of business conditions—total personal income—throughout the decade. This lends strong support to the Keynesian view that the main determinant of bank credit and the money supply was the demand for loanable funds, rather than the reserve position of banks. Further evidence in support of this proposition was the extremely low correlation between second differences of R'' and E; in a previous study by the author, the high correlation of second differences emerged as the clearest indication of causal relationship between these two variables.[14]

Despite the conclusiveness with which Horwich reported his results, the findings are, on the face of it, somewhat ambiguous. The fact is that E and R'' were positively correlated during most of the 1930's following

[12] G. Horwich, "Member Bank Effective Reserves and Earning Assets in the 'Thirties" (abstract of paper read at December 28, 1957, meeting of the Econometric Society), *Econometrica*, XXVI (October, 1958), 602–3.

[13] E. J. Kilberg, "Commercial Bank Asset Holdings and the Liquidity Trap" (doctoral thesis proposal, Department of Economics, University of Chicago, no date), pp. 4–10 (dittoed).

[14] Horwich, *loc. cit.* This argument is elaborated in G. Horwich, "Effective Reserves, Credit, and Causality in the Banking System of the 'Thirties," in D. Carson (ed.), *Banking and Monetary Studies* (Homewood, Ill.: Richard D. Irwin for U.S. Comptroller of the Currency, 1963), pp. 80–100.

the bank holiday. Horwich's contention that effective reserves exerted no causal influence on earning assets is based entirely on the failure of earning assets to exhibit a similar positive correlation with effective reserves during the 1936–38 period, when effective reserves experienced a sharp decline and then a sharp rise, as they did when effective reserves were rising steadily. In effect, Horwich permits no lag in response to changes in effective reserves, despite the fact that in an earlier application of this analytical framework, he found such lags to exist.[15] It is true that the lag was relatively short in the period covered by the earlier study. But there is little reason to suppose that the lag in response cannot be subject to significant variations from one period to another.[16] The problem of estimating the relation between R'' and E seems strikingly similar to the problem of estimating the consumption function. In both cases it may be necessary to make allowance for lags.

Horwich's evidence for the view that "the main determinant of bank credit and the money supply was the demand for loanable funds" is not convincing. It consists of a high correlation between personal income and total earning assets of banks. Horwich is himself nagged by what in my opinion seems the correct suspicion "that the causality runs from bank earning assets (and the money supply) to income, rather than conversely."[17] In correlating the money supply with personal income, Horwich found the highest correlations involved a two-quarter lag of personal income behind money—just the sort of result one would expect if money determines income, rather than vice versa. Yet Horwich attempts to say just the opposite—that income determines money (and bank earning assets)—in explaining banking behavior. The tenuous basis for this claim is that a high correlation still exists when bank earning assets are lagged slightly behind personal income. Surely a more satisfactory explanation is that if the causal connection running from money to income is strong enough, high correlations may be observed whichever variable is lagged.

Kilberg arrived at a different conclusion than Horwich did, on the basis of essentially similar data. In his analysis, he compared year-to-year changes in national bank holdings of total assets, ΔA, earning assets, ΔE, government securities, ΔG, with changes in their holdings of total reserves plus vault cash, ΔR, and vault cash plus excess reserves, ΔR_e.

---

[15] G. Horwich, "Elements of Timing and Response in the Balance Sheet of Banking, 1953–55," *Journal of Finance*, XII (May, 1957), 238–55.

[16] In his later version, Horwich admits that for the 1930's, stronger correlations between E and R'' are obtained when lags of E and R'' of one or two quarters are introduced. See *Banking and Monetary Studies, loc. cit.*

[17] *Ibid*, p. 89.

Table 1 indicates the conditions under which a liquidity trap would exist and the observed values of the test ratios, during the period 1934–41. The liquidity trap is interpreted as a situation in which banks are entirely passive with respect to increases or decreases in their reserves. For example, an increase in reserves will lead to an equal increase [18] in total assets, if the reserves are provided by a transaction that does not

TABLE 1

KILBERG'S TEST RESULTS FOR EXISTENCE OF LIQUIDITY
TRAP, NATIONAL BANKS, 1934–41

Conditions for Existence of Liquidity Trap	$\dfrac{\Delta G}{\Delta R_e}$	$\dfrac{\Delta E}{\Delta R_e}$	$\dfrac{\Delta A}{\Delta R}$
A. Change in reserves without exchange of earning assets..........	0	0	1
B. Change in reserve requirements....	0	0	d
C. Change in reserves with exchange of earning assets..................	−1	−1	0
Conditions for Non-existence of Liquidity Trap			
A. Change in reserves without exchange of earning assets..........	> 0	> 0	>1
B. Change in reserve requirements....	> 0	> 0	d
C. Change in reserves with exchange of earning assets..................	>−1	>−1	>0
Observed Values (Years Ended June 30)			
1934...............................	2.1	1.7	2.4
1935...............................	3.0	2.6	2.6
1936...............................	3.7	6.3	4.9
1937...............................	0.2c	−0.5b	2.3
1938...............................	−0.2a	−0.9a	−1.7a
1939...............................	1.2	1.8	2.1
1940...............................	0.2	0.6	1.4
1941...............................	b	b	b

a Numerator negative and denominator positive.
b Numerator positive and denominator negative.
c Numerator and denominator both negative.   d Not applicable.

involve a simultaneous exchange of assets for reserves (e.g., an inflow of gold, a deposit of currency by the public, or a transfer of Treasury deposits from the Federal Reserve to a national bank all increase reserves without a simultaneous reduction in earning assets). The other conditions can be easily derived. During most of the 1930's, gold inflows provided the bulk

[18] Kilberg's calculations eliminated cash items in process of collection and balances due from banks from total assets. Consequently, his stated conditions for the existence of a liquidity trap are only approximately correct. *Op. cit.*, p. 4.

of additions to reserves of banks. Only in 1933–34 and 1940–41 did open-market operations constitute an important source of bank reserves.

The evidence presented in Table 1 indicates a tendency for banks to respond with a lag to changes in their reserve position. In the twelve months ended June 30, 1937, banks reacted to reduced excess reserves by reducing their holdings of government securities, but total earning assets continued to increase. In the succeeding twelve months, as the volume of excess reserves again began to rise, banks were continuing to liquidate earning assets. According to Kilberg, "mid-1939–40 is the one year in which something approaching a liquidity trap condition existed, although even this year does not conform to the pure liquidity trap condition." In conclusion he stated: "These measures confirm what casual observation suggests. In no annual period from 1933–41, except during the period following a substantial administrative reduction in excess reserves, were these banks accumulating cash in an absolute sense. On the contrary, they seemed to undergo a period of rapid cash build-up soon after 1933, which seemed to be tapering off through mid-1936, before legal reserve requirements were increased."[19]

The principal weakness of Kilberg's tests is that they may merely reflect the influence of shifting demands by borrowers for loanable funds, as Horwich suggests. Without some evidence on the relation between relative interest rates and the relative proportions of different types of assets it is not entirely clear that banks were not responding passively to credit demands of borrowers.

C. Evidence from Bank Portfolios

An analysis of bank portfolio behavior and interest rates in the 1930's has been presented by Friedman and Schwartz.[20] According to them, the behavior of excess reserves during the decade from 1929–39 can be explained as part and parcel of the general hypothesis that banks' liquidity preferences shifted all along the line, away from risky assets toward liquid assets—those that an individual bank could convert into a known cash sum on short notice: "A shift in bank preferences . . . therefore explains in a simple and straightforward manner (1) the very great increase in spread for very short-term rates relative not only to long-term rates but also one-year rates; (2) the sharp shift in composition of bank port-

[19] *Ibid.*, p. 10.

[20] M. Friedman and A. Schwartz, *A Monetary History of the United States, 1867–1960* (Princeton, N.J.: Princeton University Press for the National Bureau of Economic Research, 1963), pp. 449–62.

folios; (3) the shift in the distribution of government securities among holders; and (4) the behavior of 'excess reserves.' "[21]

The objectives of Friedman and Schwartz are twofold: (*a*) to refute the hypothesis that shifts in the relative credit demands of various classes of borrowers can explain both the changes in the relative composition of bank earning asset portfolios and changes in the maturity and default risk structure of interest rates during the 1930's; and (*b*) to counter the hypothesis that in building up excess reserves, banks must have simply moved along their liquidity preference schedules in response to an increased supply of reserves.

The Friedman-Schwartz evidence against the first hypothesis can be summarized as follows:

(1) Banks increased their ratio of investments to loans (including broker's loans, commercial paper, and acceptances) despite a decline in interest rates on investments relative to interest rates on loans (including rates on commercial paper and acceptances). This cannot be explained in terms of a decrease in borrowers' demands for credit in the form of loans relative to bonded indebtedness since this would have reduced interest rates on loans relative to interest rates on investments. Consequently, there must have been a shift in bank demands away from loans toward investments. It is implied that loans as used in this comparison, are, on the whole, less liquid than investments. (2) Banks increased their holdings of short-term U.S. government securities relative to long-term U.S. government bonds, despite the fact that yields on short-term governments declined much more sharply than yields on long-term governments. A shift in relative supplies of short-term and long-term governments cannot explain both this change in the composition of bank portfolios and the change in relative interest rates. (3) Banks increased their share of the total supply of direct U.S. government obligations available for ownership by banks and the public, and their share of bills, certificates, and notes increased more than their share of bonds. This suggests that banks were shifting toward assets of greater liquidity, and that they had a stronger tendency in that direction than other investors.

Friedman and Schwartz cannot rule out the second hypothesis on the grounds of its inability to explain shifts in relative prices and quantities. The observed reduction in the spread between the yield on loans and investments and the interest yield on cash assets (excess reserves, vault cash, correspondent balances) can be explained as due to an increase in the supply of bank reserves relative to borrower demands for credit. The

[21] *Ibid.*, p. 456.

observed increase in cash assets as a proportion of bank assets (less required reserves) could therefore reflect a movement along a stable liquidity preference curve rather than a shift of it. Friedman and Schwartz content themselves with suggesting that the same kind of shifts in preferences toward greater liquidity which explain changes in the structure of non-cash bank assets and interest rates can also help explain the growth in cash assets during the 1930's. In other words, movements along a stable liquidity preference function cannot have been the whole story; there must have been some carry-over of the shifting process so clearly displayed in non-cash asset portfolio behavior.

The evidence presented by Friedman and Schwartz, while indirect, is strong presumptive backing for the view that shifts in banks' demand for cash assets did occur in the 1930's. But the explanation they give for these shifts is by no means the only one that is consistent with their evidence. We will examine their explanation and some others, in the second section of this chapter.

D. *Liquidity Preference Diagrams: Long-Term and Short-Term Rates*

Another bit of evidence that lends support to the view that banks' preferences for relatively liquid assets shifted during the 1930's is provided by comparison of Panels A and B of Figure 1. Since, by the hypothesis in question, the shift was in favor of shorter-term assets, one might expect that a liquidity preference scatter diagram would reveal such a shift better when excess reserves are plotted against long-term bond yields than when they are plotted against short-term interest rates. The reason for this is that the shift in preference as between short-term money market assets and excess reserves may have been negligible. Consequently, the excess reserves preference schedule would tend to reveal a smooth curve in which shifts, if they occurred, would be virtually indistinguishable from movements along a stable demand function.

The comparison of Panel A with Panel B confirms this reasoning. Whereas the scatter of points in Panel A tends to fall along a smooth curve relating the excess reserve ratio to short-term interest rates, this is by no means true of Panel B, in which excess reserves are related to the yield on high-quality long-term corporate bonds. The observations for the years 1932–42 show a distinct separation from the main cluster covering the years 1922–31 and 1946–58. The main cluster displays a slight but discernible negative slope suggestive of a liquidity preference function under "normal conditions." The period from 1932 to 1941 reveals itself as one in which at any given long-term interest rate, banks preferred to hold more excess reserves than they would have under normal conditions. But

EXCESS RESERVE PREFERENCES OF ALL MEMBER BANKS

AVERAGE OF JUNE AND DECEMBER CALL DATES

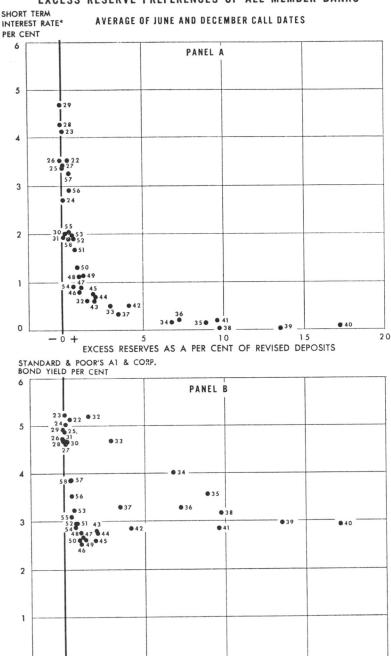

* 90 DAY BANKER'S ACCEPTANCE RATE, 1922–1934; AVG. TAXABLE EQUIVALENT YIELD ON TREASURY BILLS & CERTIFICATES, 1935–1958.

FIG. 1

while Panel B presents rather strong evidence against the existence of a liquidity trap with respect to long-term bond yields, the issue remains in doubt as concerns short-term interest rates.

E. *Comparison of Insured Member and Non-member Banks*

The dominant view of Federal Reserve officials and many others was that in the middle and late 1930's, banks were behaving passively with respect to the level of their excess reserve ratios. It was believed that after an increase in reserve requirements, member banks would not try to restore excess reserves to their original levels, but would be satisfied to let the Federal Reserve, in a word, "reclassify" excess reserves as required reserves. If this hypothesis is correct, one would not expect to find any marked divergence between the ratios of *total* reserves to deposits for country member banks and non-member banks as a result of the doubling of reserve requirements. Member banks would simply transfer reserves from the excess category to the required category and that would be the end of it. So long as both categories of banks continued to be indifferent as to whether or not they held excess reserves, the fact that non-member banks experienced no rise in their reserve requirements should not matter in the slightest insofar as the movement of the total reserve ratios are concerned.[22]

Figure 2 shows the relations between the ratio of total reserves[23] to total deposits (less cash items in process of collection) for insured non-member banks and for country member banks, the reserve class of member banks most nearly comparable with non-member banks. A comparison of the two reserve-deposit ratios does, in fact, show a divergence in movement beginning in June, 1937, as predicted by the shock hypothesis. Although the ratios of total reserves to deposits of both non-member banks and country member banks fell in the first six months of 1937, the decline was substantially greater for non-member banks, owing in part to a greater decline

---

[22] The ratio of *total* reserves to deposits is the only feasible comparison, because it is not possible to derive required reserves for non-member banks from available data. Non-member state banks are, as a rule, subject to reserve requirements imposed by state banking authorities. These vary from state to state, however, and are not strictly comparable among the various states, so that the best procedure is to make comparisons on the basis of total reserves and total deposits.

[23] Total reserves include, for present purposes, cash in vault, and balances with domestic banks—for insured non-member banks—and, in addition, reserves with Federal Reserve Banks—for country member banks. Sources: U.S. Board of Governors of the Federal Reserve System, *Member Bank Call Reports*, various issues (Washington: Board of Governors, 1934–48), and U.S. Federal Deposit Insurance Corporation, *Assets and Liabilities of Operating Insured Banks*, various issues (Washington: Federal Deposit Insurance Corporation, 1934–48).

RESERVE POSITIONS OF COUNTRY MEMBER
AND INSURED NON-MEMBER BANKS, 1934-1948
JUNE AND DECEMBER CALL DATES

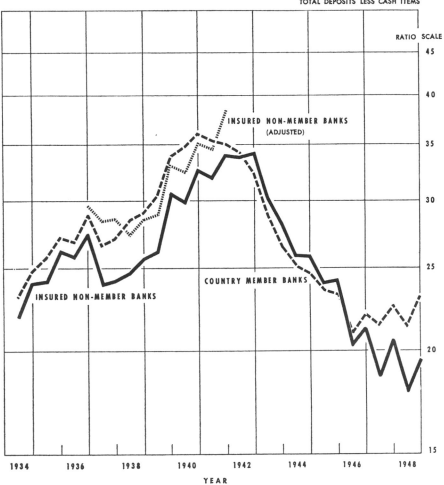

FIG. 2

in the proportion of the banking system's reserves held by the latter. This is what one would expect if country member banks were not responding in a passive manner to the reclassification of their excess reserves as required reserves, but were attempting to restore their old excess reserve ratios. Reserves tended to move toward those banks with the greatest discrepancy between their desired and their actual excess reserves. In the process, some of the banking system's cash was drawn away from non-member banks into member banks.

Suppose one asks what the total reserve ratio of insured non-member banks would have been had non-member reserve requirements been increased by the same percentage of deposits (less cash items) as was the case for country members. A crude adjustment for this may be made by adding to the reserve-deposit ratio series for non-member banks the difference between the ratio of *required* reserves to total deposits (less cash items) for country members on call dates after the first increase in reserve requirements and the corresponding ratio for country members on June 30, 1936, before the first increase in requirements. This adjusted reserve ratio for insured non-members, after an initial disparity,[24] moves roughly parallel with the reserve ratio for country member banks, between June, 1938, and June, 1941. Even more striking, the average discrepancy in this period between the country member bank reserve ratio and the adjusted ratio for non-member banks is of the same order of magnitude as it was in the period preceding the first increase in reserve requirements. Again, this is what we would expect to find if banks behaved as if their excess reserves were desired rather than redundant.

F. Bank Suspensions, 1925–32

During the 1930's, several studies were conducted on various details connected with bank failures and suspensions.[25] With few exceptions, these

[24] This disparity is caused by the inappropriateness of assuming that the adjusted reserve ratio, as constructed, will accurately depict the movements of the reserve ratio for non-members, if their required reserves were in fact increased. The initial result of an actual increase in reserve requirements would be to transfer excess reserves to the required category. Only as excess reserves are restored to levels existing before the increase in reserve requirements is our assumption valid, since it is equivalent to adding the increase in requirements to an *undisturbed* level of excess reserves. It is true that non-member banks also felt the impact of increased reserve requirements in terms of a loss of excess reserves to member banks. But it was a much milder loss than that suffered by member banks.

[25] A partial list of such studies includes: C. B. Upham and E. Lamke, *Closed and Distressed Banks* (Washington: Brookings Institution, 1934); F. L. Garlock and B. M. Gile, *Bank Failures in Arkansas*, Bulletin 315, Arkansas Agricultural Experiment Station (Fayetteville: University of Arkansas, 1935); U.S., Federal Deposit Insurance Corporation, *Annual Report, 1934* (Washington: U.S. Government Printing Office), pp.

studies gave virtually no consideration to the possibility that in an area with a high incidence of bank failure, surviving banks in the affected area might be induced to hold greater amounts of cash and other liquid assets, in relation to their deposit liabilities, as a precaution against potential runs.[26]

If suspensions did have such an effect, cross-section analysis should reveal that in Federal Reserve districts or states where suspensions were heavy, banks tended to hold larger cash reserves than banks in districts or states where the rate of suspensions was less severe, since suspension-fostered fears of the public regarding the safety of deposits would affect surviving banks near the location of a failed bank more strongly than it would affect distant banks.

A number of statistical regression tests of this hypothesis were conducted on data for Reserve Districts and states for various years between 1925 and 1932. Several variables were tested for their influence on the cash ratio, including bank size, degree of urbanization, distance from financial center, rate of change in bank cash, yields on loans and investments and correspondent balances, the ratio of time to demand deposits, and deposit instability, in addition to the rate of bank suspensions. Some regressions from this series of tests are presented in Table 2.[27]

The suspension rate shows significance at the 5 per cent level or better in all these regressions. Its significance is not markedly attenuated by the introduction of various "filtering" variables. Among all the variables tested, however, it is the distance from the nearest major financial center that consistently revealed itself to have the greatest explanatory power. By itself, the suspension rate explained at most only about one-quarter of the total variance of the excess cash ratio, and a lesser proportion of the residual variance, after allowing for the influence of the distance variable. What is more, the elasticity of the cash ratio with respect to the suspension rate is very low (.033 in the case of estimate A, when evaluated at the

---

31–73; U.S., Federal Reserve System, Committee on Branch, Group, and Chain Banking, "Bank Suspensions in the United States, 1892–1931" (Volume V of unpublished materials by the Committee, 1933); U.S., Board of Governors of the Federal Reserve System, *Federal Reserve Bulletin*, XXV (1939), 178–81, 265–70, 468–76.

[26] One exception was the Garlock and Gile study, *op. cit.*, p. 10, which indicated that, in the period 1918–30, surviving country banks in Arkansas carried reserves that were usually at least one-third greater than those of closed banks.

[27] For a fuller discussion of these tests, see G. Morrison, "Liquidity Preferences of Commercial Banks" (doctoral dissertation, Department of Economics, University of Chicago, 1963), pp. 95–109.

TABLE 2

REGRESSIONS ON MEMBER BANK CASH POSITIONS,[a] BY STATE, 1927

INDEPENDENT VARIABLE	REGRESSION COEFFICIENTS AND STANDARD ERRORS (IN PARENTHESES) OF INDEPENDENT VARIABLES Estimate		
	A	B	C
Suspension rate[b] (square root)	12.053 (5.291)	14.933 (6.467)	14.480 (5.987)
Bank size[c]	− .285 (.107)	− .213 (.162)	− .283 (.116)
Degree of urbanization[d]		− .012 (.036)	
Distance from major financial center[e]	.009 (.002)	.009 (.002)	.008 (.002)
Distance from New York[f]		.0010 (.0007)	
Rate of change in cash[g]		.074 (.057)	.042 (.049)
Yield on loans and investments[h]		.797 (1.116)	.685 (.947)
Interest yield on correspondent balances[i]			− .385 (.966)
Ratio, time deposits to net demand deposits[j]			− 2.838 (1.053)
Deposit instability[k]			.067 (.113)
Constant Term	9.016	4.543	8.321
R^2	.675	.696	.736
Number of observations[l]	49	49	49

[a] Estimate A: Excess reserves plus vault cash and due from domestic banks, as percentage of net deposits, June 30, 1927, all member banks, each state.
Estimates B and C: Excess reserves plus vault cash and due from domestic banks, as percentage of revised deposits, June 30, 1927, all member banks, each state.

[b] Ratio of deposits, all suspended commercial banks in state in year 1926 to deposits of all commercial banks operating on June 30 of 1926.

[c] Average size of member banks in state in terms of total assets, millions of dollars, June 30, 1927.

[d] Percentage of state population living in cities of 25,000 and over. A weighted average of figures for 1920 and 1930 is the basis for the percentage calculation: Percentages for 1920 are weighted 1/4; percentages for 1930 are weighted 3/4.

[e] Distance of principal financial center of each state to nearest major financial center (New York, Chicago, Boston, or San Francisco), in statute miles.

[f] Distance of principal financial center of each state to New York City, in statute miles.

[g] Percentage change in total reserves plus vault cash and due from domestic banks, March 23, 1927, to June 30, 1927, member banks.

[h] Annual rate of earnings on loans and investments, six months ended June 30, 1927, as percentage of total loans and investments, March 23, 1927, national banks, each state.

[i] Interest on balances due from domestic banks, for national banks, six months ended June 30, 1927, divided by the sum of cash in vault, excess reserves and balances due from banks, for national banks, March 23, 1927, each state. Multiplied by two to put the figures on an annual rate basis.

[j] Ratio, time deposits, all member banks to net demand deposits, all member banks, June 30, 1927, each state.

[k] Ratio of the standard error of estimate (adjusted for degrees of freedom) of D_{jt} (total deposits, all commercial banks, state j, June 30 of year t) in the regression $D_{jt} = a + \beta t$ (t runs from 1921 through 1927) to the mean of D_{jt} over the period 1921–27.

[l] Includes forty-eight states and the District of Columbia.

means of the two variables). A doubling of the suspension rate would lead to only a 3 per cent increase in the cash ratio.

An attempt was made to see whether differences among Federal Reserve Districts in the role of bank suspensions during the crisis years, 1931–33, could explain differences in cash ratios among Federal Reserve districts for years subsequent to the crisis. The results were adverse to the suspension hypothesis. But when the banking system is generally afflicted with financial distress, the effects of bank suspensions cease to be localized.

Perhaps, under these conditions, the most relevant cross-sectional studies will be those that are international in scope. An example of this is the striking comparison of Canadian and U.S. banking experience presented in the following chapter. Like most of the evidence examined in this chapter, it lends support to the view that during the 1930's bank liquidity preference schedules were shifting toward greater holdings of cash.

FACTORS THAT MIGHT HAVE CAUSED SHIFTS IN BANK LIQUIDITY PREFERENCES

The evidence presented in the previous section points rather clearly to the existence of shifts in bank liquidity preferences during the 1930's, but much less clearly to the forces that could have induced banks to want to hold more cash even if interest rates had not declined. A lengthy if artifical list of possible technologically based shifts can, of course, be constructed. But the factors of bona fide relevance to the conditions of the 1930's seem to fall into two broadly distinct categories—those factors related to the cost of holding or borrowing money and those that were a direct legacy of the banking crisis. In a remarkable passage,[28] Leonard Ayres, economist of the Cleveland Trust Company, succinctly stated these two main themes:

> Probably it is true that in two important respects bankers as a class are still unduly influenced by developments that lie in the past, and that are not at all likely to recur. Both of them appear to be misleading inferences based on past experience. One of them is an optimistic hope and the other is a pessimistic fear.
>
> The optimistic hope is that as business recovery continues we shall once more have the old volumes of commercial loans. The reason why that hope is unwarranted is that commercial loans were abnormally large in the 1920's while businesses were short of working capital, due to the wartime advances in price levels. The loans shrunk rapidly towards the end of the prosperity period as business increased its working capital. The volume of trade has already regained

---

[28] L. P. Ayres, "Prospects for Profits in the Banking Business," *The Commercial and Financial Chronicle*, American Bankers Convention Section, October 30, 1937, p. 28.

the levels of 1925 but the commercial loans now are only about one-third as large as they were then . . .

The pessimistic fear that bankers still cherish, and by which they guide their policies, is that we may have another banking crisis like the one five years ago. The fear explains our passion for liquidity. It is the chief reason for the excess reserves that we maintain. It is behind our preference for short-term notes, and our abhorrence for long-term bonds. It is the reason why most bankers are completely reluctant to contemplate borrowing from their Federal Reserve Banks.

Ayres urged banks to "devote increasing attention to their investment accounts" with the aim of "securing the fuller investment of the available funds of banks."[29]

A. *Cost of Holding or Borrowing Money*

The basic notion here is that market interest rates on bank earning assets may not accurately reflect the true cost of holding money and may neglect entirely the cost of borrowing money. A curve depicting bank demand for cash as a function of market interest rates may be unstable (i.e., may shift) insofar as these neglected cost factors vary. The two ways in which the cost of holding money needs to be modified are with respect to interest rate expectations and default risk expectations. If interest rates are expected to rise, or if an increasing proportion of borrowers are expected to fail to repay interest or principal, expectations of capital losses are generated and the true expected yields on long-term defaultable assets are less than their observed market yields. Consequently, the bank demand for cash would be greater at any given market yield than if these adverse expectations were absent.

During the 1930's, in particular, such expectations were believed to be prevalent among bankers. For example, changing expectations of higher interest rates are the basis of the explanation of bank reserve positions in the later 1930's offered by Samuelson and discussed in the previous chapter.[30] If this hypothesis is valid, a variable purporting to measure interest rate expectations, such as the spread between long-term and short-term interest rates should do a good job of explaining apparent shifts in the

[29] L. P. Ayres, "Report of the Economic Policy Commission," *ibid.*, p. 29.

[30] It may be puzzling how a factor which is sometimes given credit for producing liquidity traps can also be regarded merely as a demand shift factor. The liquidity trap version arises when there is an assumed rigid inverse relation between the level of current market yields and expected rates of change in interest rates, such that one or the other variable, is adequate to explain liquidity preferences.

liquidity preference schedule of banks. Similarly, there is no lack of evidence that bank loans and investments were subject to unusually high rates of loss through default during the 1930's. If, in fact, banks made allowance for increased expected default risks, one would suppose that a measure of default risk premiums, such as the spread between yields on bonds of different grade, would catch the effect of changing expectations of defaults on shifts in liquidity preferences.

The difficulty with both of these measures of expectations is that yield spreads may change for reasons other than changes in the expectations in question. Lenders may become more cautious, that is, become increasingly averse to taking risks, for reasons that are related to, but not identical with, their interest rate or default expectations. In a war or in a severe depression, increased uncertainty on a broad front may shift the public's preferences toward liquid assets in such a way as to widen the yield spreads between long-term and short-term or low-grade and high-grade bonds without any help from changing expectations about future interest rates or default rates. Accordingly, empirical findings that liquidity preferences are shifted by changes in these yield spreads is inconclusive evidence for the specific expectational hypotheses being examined.

There is a different sort of ambiguity about the role of borrowing costs on the demand for cash. If these costs rise in relation to the yields on earning assets, bank demand for cash should increase since borrowing to meet unexpected cash needs would then be a more expensive substitute for holding cash itself. For eleven years, beginning in October, 1931, with the raising of the New York Federal Reserve Bank's discount rate to 3.5 per cent, the cost of borrowing from the Federal Reserve exceeded many if not most short-term money market interest rates, sometimes by wide margins. As a factor that may have contributed to the shifting of bank liquidity preferences, the discount rate cannot be overlooked. But it is not clear that the discount rate itself accurately measures the penalty costs associated with borrowing. First of all, there are other markets for loans to banks, notably Federal Funds. More important, the Federal Reserve has long operated the discount window on the presumption that borrowing is "a privilege, not a right," i.e., on a basis of limited direct access of individual banks to borrowed funds. The limitations may be viewed as an implicit component of the cost of borrowed money. But the rationing criteria, based on evaluations of individual bank "needs," have been uniform neither from year-to-year nor from Reserve Bank-to-Reserve Bank. The discount rate may therefore be a very crude approximation to the true penalty cost we seek.

B. Banking Crisis and Its Effects on Liquidity Preferences

There are a number of aspects of the banking crisis of the 1930's that, in leaving their mark on the subsequent banking environment, may have caused shifts in bank demand for excess reserves. Approximately nine thousand banks failed in the four years, 1930–33, and in the aftermath of the worst bank panic in U.S. history, it would not be surprising to find the surviving banks exercising extreme caution in their lending and investment policies so as to increase their liquidity and prevent impairment of their capital positions.[31] Virtual abdication by the Federal Reserve of its responsibilities under the Federal Reserve Act as a "lender of last resort," during the bank panic of the early 1930's, impressed on banks the need to rely on their own devices to survive any recurrence of liquidity crisis.[32] Bank examiners came under criticism during the 1930's for excessive conservatism in evaluating the quality of banks' assets[33] and for several years

[31] The interdependence of bank liquidity and bank solvency during and after a bank panic led one writer to turn the Keynesian liquidity trap hypothesis upside down: "As the security of bank deposits is now impaired by the losses the bank has sustained, the latter may now choose to compensate its depositors for diminished safety by increased liquidity. . . . But this will, of course, only be necessary if the capital of the banks is not immediately reconstructed; for in the latter case, the security of the deposits will at once be restored. Now there is one good reason why we should expect the banks to go in for increased liquidity rather than for immediate reconstruction . . . the rate of interest is likely to be very high during the period under consideration. The new capital which has to be borrowed for the sake of reconstruction will therefore be relatively expensive, and it is quite natural that the owners of the banks should try to postpone this operation to a point of time when new capital will be cheaper. But as . . . depositors must be compensated somehow, the banks will in the meantime have to raise the cash proportion of their assets. Contrary to Mr. Keynes' theory, we find that it is the expectation of a future *lower* rate of interest which, because of the increased uncertainty of the banks, leads to enhanced liquidity preference."

The writer, of course, neglects the possibility that expectations of higher rates of interest on bank assets may coexist with expectations of lower costs of obtaining bank capital. L. M. Lachmann, "Uncertainty and Liquidity-Preference," *Economica* (New Series), IV (August, 1937), 295–308.

[32] I should like to thank Dr. Clark Warburton for emphasizing this to me. As he points out, the Federal Reserve moved, in the space of a little more than ten years, from a discount policy of extreme laxity (in 1918–19) to one of severe restrictiveness (in 1931–33).

[33] In 1936, Jacob Viner had this to say about the peculiarities of examiner psychology: "The nature of the examining process is itself such as to impose upon the activities of the bank a perverse cyclical pattern from the point of view of stabilization. . . . When business is prosperous and optimism prevails, examiners, like bankers themselves, must tend to appraise credit risks in terms of the favorable conditions of the moment. . . . Later, when the tide of business turns, when banks begin to fail and loans which were passed without criticism during the boom days have to be written off as bad debts, the examiners are blamed. Reacting in a perfectly natural manner, they become stricter and more exacting in the standards they apply, and they press the banks to liquidate loans

after the 1933 bank holiday discouraged aggressive credit extension by banks.[34] Later, the drastic doubling of reserve requirements in 1936–37, undertaken on the presumption that banks did not really need or want to hold large amounts of excess reserves, could be expected to induce banks to take renewed precautions to build up an additional buffer of liquid assets as protection against repetitions of a misguided monetary policy.

Unfortunately, none of these environmental influences seems susceptible of direct testing. The volume of bank suspensions in the 1930's does not correlate well with excess reserve ratios either temporally or cross-sectionally. Prospects for measuring variations in the stringency of bank examination or in the willingness of the Federal Reserve to extend discount privileges are lost in the shroud of confidentiality that surrounds these supervisory functions. The doubling of reserve requirements is a unique event in our monetary annals; one observation rarely constitutes convincing evidence in favor of any hypothesis.

Indirect verification of these crisis-centered forces is possible, however. The procedure involves specifying certain models of response that one might expect banks to follow when subjected to the typical stresses of a bank panic or liquidity crisis. The tests, then, will determine whether banks adhere to the response pattern of a given model. Failure to find evidence for a particular response pattern need not be considered fatal to

and investments which the banks if left to their own devices, would be happy to keep in their portfolios." J. Viner, "Recent Legislation and the Banking Situation," *American Economic Review, Papers and Proceedings*, XXVI (March, 1936), 109.

[34] The U.S., Federal Deposit Insurance Corporation, *Annual Report, 1936* (Washington: U.S. Government Printing Office, 1937), p. 19, contains the following warning: "When a bank buys securities with the primary intention of selling them again at higher prices, that bank is speculating. Dealing in high-grade securities does not alter the essential speculative nature of the transaction. . . .

"Over the past few years, some banks have been using profits secured from speculation in securities to pay dividends and to retire preferred stock without making adequate provision for possible future depreciation in the securities purchased by them at high levels of prices. . . . The Corporation insists that insured banks should make provision for any depreciation or losses that may occur. To fail to make such provision is to engage in an unsound banking practice."

It was not until the summer of 1938 that the federal and state examining authorities agreed to shelve the much abused "slow" loans classification of examiner's reports. According to Homer Jones: "There has been a tendency to place in this category any loans considered not to conform to the self-liquidating loan theory of commercial banking. The 1938 agreement provided that the category formerly designated as "slow" should henceforth have merely a numerical designation and should include only loans involving 'a substantial and unreasonable degree of risk to the bank.' " H. Jones, "An Appraisal of the Rules and Procedures of Bank Supervision, 1929–39," *Journal of Political Economy*, XLVIII (April, 1940), 193.

the basic liquidity crisis hypothesis. Conversely, strong evidence for the existence of a particular response pattern need not be considered equally strong evidence for the basic hypothesis.

Two possible patterns of bank response to liquidity crisis will be developed and tested in this study. One will be termed the "shock" effect, the other the "inertia" effect.

i. The Shock Effect

Banks might be shocked into desiring a sharply higher level of excess reserves and other liquid assets during a liquidity crisis. Gradually, as memory of the crisis fades, and provided no new shocks occur, banks would desire to return to a more normal level of excess reserves. The shock model could be interpreted as a highly particularized version of the factors determining expected cash drain, $\bar{v}$, as defined in Chapter II. In a crisis or panic, banks immediately want to hold greatly increased amounts of cash because they have been shocked into expecting very large cash drains. But it might also be that the crisis evokes greater uncertainty or dispersion of expected cash drains and that this produces the change in desired excess reserves.[35]

Banks, however, may be either unwilling or unable to move immediately to their desired level of cash reserves. The immediate attainment of such a goal would require liquidation of secondary reserve assets or even loans on unfavorable terms. Rapid liquidation at depressed asset prices might even force the bank into receivership through impairment of its capital. Moreover, since the bank might well prefer to hang on to its relatively liquid earning assets, the burden of attaining a stronger cash and liquid assets position may tend to be borne by sale of longer term investments and reduction of loans. This is likely to be a lengthy, drawn-out process. The losses on quick sale of long-term investments could be substantial, while in the case of loans, liquidation without default on the part of the borrower may entail repayment over an extended period. For these reasons, the attainment of a higher desired level of cash may proceed over many months.

The statistical application of this shock model to actual fluctuations in excess reserves will be more fully developed in later chapters. It will suffice for present purposes to illustrate how it might operate. Observe, in Figure 3, that the excess reserve ratio of New York banks builds up after the bank holiday, reaches a peak at the end of 1935, and then starts to

[35] As will be recalled, the bank profit maximization theory of Chapter II lent little support to this interpretation. But under an appropriate risk aversion theory this explanation might carry more weight.

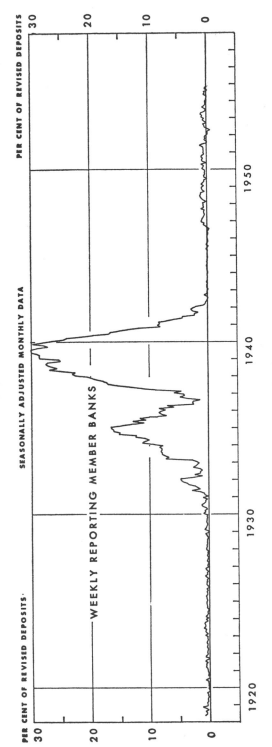

EXCESS RESERVE RATIO OF NEW YORK BANKS
1919-1955

FIG. 3

decline before the first increase in reserve requirements in August, 1936. Following the last of the three increases in requirements in May, 1937, the excess reserve ratio started an upward movement that was maintained, with only minor interruptions until the last six months of 1940. Thereafter the ratio fell abruptly in the next two years to extremely low wartime levels.

This pattern of fluctuation is of the general form one might expect if desired cash positions jumped to much higher levels during periods of shock in 1931–33 and 1936–37, and then generally declined, while actual cash positions only slowly approached desired levels. This is precisely the explanation offered by Friedman and Schwartz. "The first shift [in bank liquidity preferences] occurred as a result of the experience during 1929–33, and the adaptation took about three years, from 1933 to 1936. The second occurred as a result of the successive rises in reserve requirements, reinforced by the occurrence of a severe contraction that was a stern reminder of earlier experience. The adaptation to it took about the same length of time, from 1937 to 1940."[36]

A rough schematic illustration of how the shock effect may have operated is shown in Figure 4. Except for the periods immediately following each shock, desired and actual excess reserve ratios are assumed to be equal. The shocks, dated at the beginning of 1933 and 1937, cause the desired ratio to jump by a multiple of the actual reserve ratio existing at the time of the shock. But these shock effects gradually dissipate, as depicted by the dotted line labeled "desired excess reserve ratio." Actual reserve ratios only gradually approach the desired ratios, taking about three years to restore equilibrium. The resulting hypothetical pattern approximates the grosser movements of the observed excess reserve ratio as shown in Figure 3. The fit may be improved by taking into account changes in interest rates and short-term fluctuations in total bank reserves, which in 1933 and 1937 may have temporarily prevented banks from moving toward the desired reserve ratio.

ii. The Inertia Effect of Banking Crises

One of the principal consequences of bank panics or liquidity crises may be to induce in surviving banks a heightened sense of caution in all their activities, especially the granting of credit. Under normal circumstances, banks may react rather quickly to changes in their capacity to create deposits by making new loans and investments. Increases or decreases in reserves and reserve requirements will be followed fairly rapidly by adjustments in the volume of earning assets and bank deposits. Excess

[36] Friedman and Schwartz, *op. cit.*, p. 538.

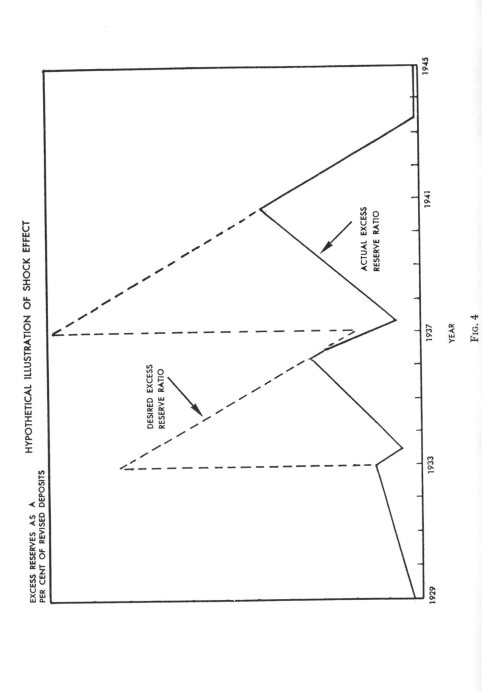

EXCESS RESERVES AS A
PER CENT OF REVISED DEPOSITS

HYPOTHETICAL ILLUSTRATION OF SHOCK EFFECT

DESIRED EXCESS
RESERVE RATIO

ACTUAL EXCESS
RESERVE RATIO

1929   1933   1937   1941   1945

YEAR

FIG. 4

reserves will not fluctuate greatly because banks have reasonable confidence that a change in deposit-creating potential which persists for a very moderate length of time will not be quickly reversed. In other words, the normal state of affairs is that from the point of view of bank expectations, the banks' current level of deposit-creating potential (bank reserves adjusted for changes in reserve requirements, as defined in Chapter II) and their long-run, expected, or "permanent" level of deposit potential do not diverge widely, because the expected level is rapidly revised to recognize changes in the current level.

But under the impact of bank panic, sharp fluctuations in the volume of reserves, large changes in reserve requirements, or other forces putting extreme pressure on the banking system's liquid resources, banks may revise their horizon for estimating the permanent level of deposit potential, placing less confidence in their current experience. A large proportion of a current increase or decrease in potential deposits may be regarded by banks as too temporary to warrant a corresponding change in actual deposits (except insofar as is necessary to meet reserve requirements). Banks may only reluctantly let these transitory movements in potential deposits be the basis for changes in bank credit, and may prefer, in whatever asset adjustments they do make, to confine them to the purchase and sale of liquid assets—marketable securities instead of loans, short-term rather than long-term instruments.[37]

The essence of this variant of the shift hypothesis is that in the aftermath of bank panics or liquidity crises, the expectational horizon of banks lengthens and this tends to break the normally close link between current deposit potential and actual bank deposits. It is replaced by a more or less close link between movements of deposit potential and the excess reserve ratio—one that does not exist except in the very shortest run under calmer conditions.

The relation between total potential deposits (total reserves divided by average required reserve ratio) and the excess reserve ratio for weekly reporting New York City banks is shown in Figure 5. It will be observed that during the 1930's, the two series tend to move upward and downward together, whereas in other periods the relationship is much less pronounced. Under the shock hypothesis, the co-movement of the two series would be considered to be *mostly* a matter of coincidence.[38] The chart

[37] A version of this hypothesis has recently been endorsed in A. Meltzer and K. Brunner, *An Alternative Approach to the Monetary Mechanism*, U.S., Congress, House, Committee on Banking and Currency, 88th cong., 2d Sess., August 17, 1964, pp. 2–7.

[38] That more than coincidence is involved may be inferred from the similar short-run pattern of movement of the two series for New York Clearing House Banks during the period 1874–1913. See Figure 7, *infra*.

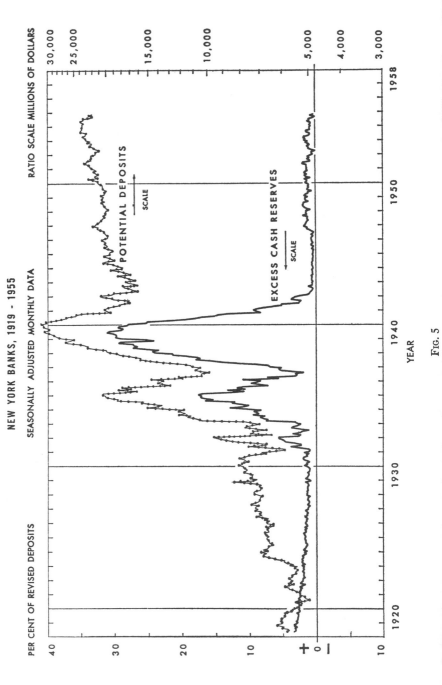

EXCESS CASH RESERVE RATIO AND POTENTIAL DEPOSITS

NEW YORK BANKS, 1919 - 1955

SEASONALLY ADJUSTED MONTHLY DATA

PER CENT OF REVISED DEPOSITS

RATIO SCALE MILLIONS OF DOLLARS

POTENTIAL DEPOSITS
SCALE

EXCESS CASH RESERVES
SCALE

YEAR

Fig. 5

suggests that if lags in response of banks to changes in reserves are at the root of the explanation of the large volume of excess reserves that banks held during the middle and late 1930's, the time lag for banks was a good deal greater during the 1930's than in periods before and after, and greater than other investigators have come to believe.

It is worth emphasizing that the explanation in terms of lags in expectational response to potential deposits is an application of the notion of expected cash drain introduced in Chapter II. The connection lies in the hypothesis that on the basis of past movements in total deposit potential, banks form expectations as to the "permanent" level of their potential deposits and that positive deviations of current potential deposits from their "permanent" level (i.e., positive transitory potential deposits) are equivalent to an expectation, by banks, that they are likely to suffer cash drains (and, conversely, in the case of a negative deviation).

In this terminology the inertia of banks has to do with the manner in which banks form estimates of their permanent potential deposits on the basis of past experience. A different sort of inertia is an integral part of the shock hypothesis—the inertia of slow closure of the gap between desired and actual reserve positions. A more comprehensive framework of analysis could combine the two effects. For example, one can conceive of the crisis shock causing a gap between desired and actual cash, which is closed at a rate that is a function of transitory potential deposits. The main reason for not exploring this possibility is that it leads to a rather unwieldy model, one in which expectational and "adjustment" lags are not readily distinguishable by statistical methods.

SUMMARY

There are several grounds on which the liquidity trap explanation of bank behavior during the 1930's may be questioned. They include:

1) Borrower complains about unavailability of bank credit.

2) Responsiveness (albeit with a lag) of bank loans and investments to increases in reserve availability.

3) Changes in the structure of bank portfolios that cannot be explained merely by changes in borrower demand for various types of credit.

4) Failure of a scatter diagram of excess reserve ratios plotted against bond yields clearly to show a possible liquidity trap.

5) Differences between member banks and non-member banks in response to the 1936–37 increase in reserve requirements—differences that cannot be reconciled with the liquidity trap hypothesis.

6) The effect of cross-sectional variations in bank suspension rates on

bank cash positions in pre-crisis years supports the alternative to the liquidity trap hypothesis, namely, shifts in bank liquidity preferences.

When reinforced by the comparison with Canadian banking presented in the following chapter, these bits of evidence make it very difficult to accept the notion that banks in the 1930's regarded the level of their excess reserves with indifference.

A fully convincing refutation of the liquidity trap hypothesis, however, requires something more than negative evidence. There is needed a cogent alternative explanation for the unusual heights to which excess reserves rose in the decade of the great depression; such an explanation presumably depends on postulated shifts in the liquidity preference curve of the banking system. The main candidates among factors that could have caused such shifts are (a) influences related to the cost of holding or borrowing money, and (b) bank attitudes that may have developed as the direct aftermath of the liquidity crises of the 1930's. Among possible attitudes, two conceptually distinct variants, the "shock" effect and the "inertia" effect, appear amenable to empirical tests. The results of these tests will be reported in later chapters.

V

Canadian Experience

IF BANKS in the United States in fact held huge volumes of excess cash reserves in the decade of the 1930's because of a dearth of investment opportunities, we should expect banks in countries similarly beset by business depression to behave in a like manner. By this standard, Canada offers an almost ideal example for comparison, inasmuch as the amplitudes and timing of fluctuations in business activity were roughly the same in each country. Constant dollar gross national product declined by 29 per cent in both countries between 1929–33, then rose by 63 per cent in the United States and by 72 per cent in Canada between 1933–40. In terms of current prices, GNP fell by 46 per cent in the United States and by 43 per cent in Canada from 1929–33. It then increased by 80 per cent and 92 per cent, respectively, during the 1933–40 period.[1] As will be seen later, movements of interest rates in the two countries were much the same in the period under consideration. Thus, if the economic situation was ripe for the development of a banker's liquidity trap in the United States, the same can be said for Canada.

Canada, of course, entered World War II more than two years before the United States, and we would be remiss not to take note of certain other important differences influencing the banking conditions of the two countries. One of these differences is a distinct blessing from the standpoint of our analysis. For unlike the United States, the Canadian banking system experienced no bank failures during the 1930's and no significant runs on banks. In fact, the history of Canadian banking is almost entirely free of serious bank panics. In all, there have been only 32 bank failures since 1822 and none whatsoever since 1923. The total losses to depositors have amounted to a mere $20 million in nearly 160 years.[2] This absence of a panic environment presents so extreme a contrast to the unsettling circumstances in U.S. banking during the 1930's as virtually to create the conditions of a controlled economic experiment. Under the liquidity crisis

[1] Sources: U.S., Bureau of the Census, *Historical Statistics of the United States* (Washington: U.S. Government Printing Office, 1960), p. 139; Canada, Dominion Bureau of Statistics, *Canadian Statistical Review*, 1959 Supplement (Ottawa: The Queen's Printer and Controller of Stationery, 1959), pp. 13, 15.

[2] E. L. Stewart Patterson, *Canadian Banking* (Toronto: Ryerson Press, 1932), p. 317.

hypothesis that has been presented as an alternative to the liquidity trap, there is no reason to suppose Canadian banks would have accumulated unusually large amounts of cash during the 1930's.

The Canadian banking structure also differs from that of the United States during the period of major interest in this study in that there were fewer than twenty banks in Canada, each administering networks of branches extending across wide areas of the nation. Branch banking has been strong since the early nineteenth century, and it is in large part because of the size and strength of these branch systems that Canada has experienced few bank failures. Weaker institutions, as a rule, have been merged into the stronger ones, and in the process, there has been a gradual reduction in the number of chartered banks.

Another difference between the two systems, at least until recently, has been the role played by legal reserve requirements. Before enactment of the Bank of Canada Act of 1935, chartered banks were not subject to legal reserve requirements against deposit liabilities. In addition to establishing a central bank,[3] the act set a 5 per cent required reserve against deposits in Canada, the reserves to be held in Canada in the form of Bank of Canada deposits or notes. The chartered banks however, had conventionally held a minimum cash reserve substantially in excess of the required 5 per cent. The imposition of this legal requirement had little perceptible effect on the actual cash ratio.

The conventional minimum cash reserve ratio has a lengthy, if somewhat cloudy history in Canadian banking practice. The specific rules of thumb followed by the chartered banks have apparently been modified somewhat over the years. According to testimony received by the U.S. National Monetary Commission, the usual practice in the first decade of this century was to keep a 15 per cent reserve against deposits, 8 to 10

---

[3] Under the Finance Acts of 1914 and 1923, the Minister of Finance acquired a limited central banking power to make advances, in the form of Dominion Notes, to chartered banks and to determine the interest rates to be charged for such borrowing. This had important economic consequences, but it is mentioned here primarily because it paved the way to a form of "window dressing" by the chartered banks. The banks, being required to report their condition to the Minister of Finance each month end, arranged to inflate their cash for reporting purposes by large month-end borrowings of Dominion Notes. As suggested by Plumptre, it is possible to correct for such window dressing by substituting an estimate of monthly average bank holdings of Dominion Notes for the reported month-end figures. This type of window dressing declined in the early 1930's and ceased entirely with the advent of the Bank of Canada. The chartered banks continued to window dress their annual reports, but this has only a minor effect on annual average data. See A. F. W. Plumptre, *Central Banking in the British Dominions* (Toronto: University of Toronto Press, 1947), pp. 238–40. See also, Canada, *Report of the Royal Commission on Banking and Currency, 1933* (Ottawa: King's Printer, 1933), pp. 41–43.

per cent of which was to be in vault cash, the remainder to be balances
with other banks and liquid securities. Apparently, the Canadian Bankers'
Association was the principal agency enforcing this gentlemen's agreement.[4] Under Canadian law the Association has certain regulatory pow-
ers, most important of which is the supervision of clearing houses.[5] The
reserve ratio was not, however, held perfectly constant in succeeding
years. Plumptre notes that the proportion ran up to more than 15 per
cent in World War I, was slightly below 10 per cent in the boom of 1920,
and was below 8 per cent in 1929.[6] By the early 1930's, the banks had
settled on a 10 per cent minimum, supposedly to be composed of vault
cash and balances with banks.[7] In practice, however, the banks appear
for many years to have maintained very close to the full 10 per cent in
vault cash or balances in the "Central Gold Reserve" (later replaced by
Bank of Canada deposits).[8] In July, 1954, the legal reserve requirement
was raised to 8 per cent of deposits in Canada. This change, which on the
surface appeared to be an increase in legal reserve requirements, turned
out to be a decrease in effective reserve requirements. First, the 10 per cent
convention was abandoned. Second, the chartered banks previously had
been legally required to maintain a 5 per cent reserve *each day* against the
monthly average of deposits for the second preceding month; the banks
now have only to maintain a *monthly average* of 8 per cent against the
average of deposits for four successive Wednesdays, ending with the
second to last Wednesday of the previous month.[9] The chartered banks
are thereby given considerable latitude in adjusting their reserve positions
on an intra-month basis, and the banks may regard this computational

[4] U.S., National Monetary Commission, *Interviews on the Banking and Currency
Systems of Canada*, 61st Cong., 2d Sess. (Washington: U.S. Government Printing Office,
1910), *passim;* J. F. Johnson, *The Canadian Banking System* (Washington: U.S. Government Printing Office, 1910), p. 71.

[5] R. C. McIvor, *Canadian Monetary, Banking, and Fiscal Development* (Toronto:
Macmillan Co., 1958), p. 78.

[6] Plumptre, *op. cit.*, p. 238. Plumptre's figures understate the true cash ratio because
they exclude chartered bank deposits in the Central Gold Reserve.

[7] J. H. Creighton, *Central Banking in Canada* (Vancouver, B.C.: Clarke & Stuart
Co., 1933), p. 84; M. L. Stokes, *The Bank of Canada* (Toronto: Macmillan Co., 1939),
p. 8; B. H. Beckhart, *The Banking System of Canada* (New York: Henry Holt & Co.,
1929), p. 430.

[8] McIvor, *op. cit.*, p. 228; A. B. Jamieson, *Chartered Banking in Canada* (Toronto:
Ryerson Press, 1953), p. 185.

[9] E. P. Neufeld, *Bank of Canada Operations and Policy* (Toronto: University of
Toronto Press, 1958), p. 55; Bank of Canada, *Statistical Summary, Financial Supplement, 1958* (Ottawa: Bank of Canada, 1959), p. 16. Till money held on the four Wednesdays counts toward meeting reserve requirements.

procedure as affording them much the same degree of flexibility as they had under the old self-imposed 10 per cent convention.[10]

Despite the vagaries of the term "reserve requirements" as applied to Canadian banking, the most reasonable approximation clearly seems to be to assume a 10 per cent reserve ratio before July 1, 1954, and 8 per cent thereafter. Although our purpose in doing this is to compare excess reserves of Canadian banks with those of United States banks, it should be evident from the foregoing discussion that except possibly for recent years, the term "reserve requirement" denotes a more hazy and flexible constraint on bank behavior in Canada than it does in the United States. As it turns out, however, the results of our comparison depend very little on the precise definition of required reserves one might choose to apply.

Another somewhat troublesome difference between Canada and the United States is the absence, for most of the period we shall study, of an effective short-term money market in the former country. In the 1920's, Canadian banks relied heavily on the New York call loan, bankers' acceptance, and commercial paper markets as outlets for short-term lending. To a lesser extent, the banks sent funds to the London money market. Loans to the stock markets in Canada generally have been handled on much the same sort of personal basis as ordinary business loans and have been call loans in name only. No published time series of call loan rates is available. The same applies to commercial paper, until recent years, at least. During the early 1930's, short-term government securities tended to replace call loans as the principal instrument in U.S. money market transactions. The tax exemption accorded U.S. investors in government securities depressed their yields and made them relatively unsuitable for Canadian bank investment. Although continuing to rely on the New York money market to some extent, the chartered banks came increasingly to employ the new Canadian three-month Treasury bills in adjusting their reserve positions. These were first issued by the government in 1934. Starting in 1935, the Bank of Canada bought and sold these bills, dealing almost exclusively with banks. Although this arrangement greatly enhanced the marketability of Canadian bills, it did not create a Canadian money market in the strict sense of the word.[11] For various reasons, most notably its desire to obtain a better "feel" of changes in credit conditions, the Bank in 1953 and 1954 took steps to create such a money market. It widened the spread between its bid and ask prices on bills, introduced discount rate schedules that penalize banks for overly frequent or exces-

---

[10] On the other hand, the banks cannot quickly alter the amount of their required reserves by changing the volume of their deposits.

[11] Plumptre, *op. cit.*, pp. 140–43, 327–32.

sive borrowing, and discouraged the chartered banks from direct bill transactions with the Bank of Canada by discountinuing the practice of immediate cash settlement on such transactions. The last measure was decisive, and in June, 1954, there sprang up a money market in bills tailored to the Bank of Canada's liking. The Bank became a "lender of last resort" for securities dealers, on the pattern of the Bank of England, and a new money market instrument came into being—the "day to day" loans by chartered banks to securities dealers.[12]

The varied and shifting loci of short-term lending by chartered banks in the past few decades hampers the selection of a time series of interest rates to measure the cost to Canadian banks of holding excess reserves. In view of the lessening importance of the New York money market to these banks, it appears that the Canadian bill rate is the best choice for the period since 1935. For the late 1920's, the New York call loan rate is certainly a relevant possibility, but we have chosen the rate on ninety-day prime bankers' acceptances, since the eligibility for rediscount, tax status, and maturity of this instrument makes it more comparable to the later Canadian bill. For the early 1930's, the choice of a suitable rate is rendered more difficult by the transitional state of the New York money market mentioned previously. Probably the bankers' acceptance rate is as representative as any short rate in this troubled period.[13]

Aside from these major dissimilarities between the two banking systems, there are, of course, certain differences in the characteristics of deposit liabilities[14] and differences in the kinds and amounts of assets in which banks can invest.[15] But these disparities do not seem sufficiently

---

[12] Neufeld, *op. cit.*, pp. 52–57. Also see B. K. MacLaury, "The Canadian Money Market, Its Development and Its Impact" (doctoral dissertation, Department of Economics, Harvard University, 1961).

[13] From the point of view of a Canadian investor accustomed to operating in the New York money market, the interest rate implied by the spread between the spot and forward Canadian–U.S. exchange rates should also be taken into account. The market in forward exchange affords an opportunity for hedging against fluctuations in the spot exchange rate that would otherwise introduce an element of uncertainty into the net Canadian dollar equivalent of the interest rate in New York. Our principal reason for neglecting this refinement is the unavailability of data on forward Canadian exchange rates for the period in question.

[14] "Notice" deposits, for example, are generally similar to our savings deposits, except that it has been customary to permit limited checking privileges on them. Plumptre, *op. cit.*, p. 126.

[15] One difference is that before passage of the National Housing Act of 1954, chartered banks were prohibited from making loans on real estate and could hold mortgages only on assignment arising from a previously existing loan. Also, Canadian banks are permitted to invest in and act as dealers in corporate bonds and stocks. See Jamieson, *op. cit.*, pp. 186, 296. A recent innovation is the requirement that chartered banks main-

pronounced to have a significant bearing on the issues with which we are presently concerned.[16]

Let us turn then to the comparison of the liquidity preferences of Canadian and United States banks. (See Table 3 and Figure 6.) New York City weekly reporting member banks have been chosen for this comparison because they are more nearly similar in size to the Canadian chartered banks than are U.S. member banks as a whole. Looking first at the chartered banks' excess reserve ratio, we should expect to discern some tendency for the ratio to be relatively high at low interest rates particularly if the liquidity trap hypothesis is valid.

It is reasonably clear that such a tendency can be observed, but its magnitude is undoubtedly exaggerated by the observations for 1927 through 1932. Between this early period and the years 1953 through 1958, there occurred an obvious shift of preferences for excess reserves by Canadian banks. At corresponding interest rates it appears that these banks desired to maintain excess reserve ratios approximately 2.5 percentage points higher in the later period than in the earlier one.

There are several reasons for thinking that this shift actually took place between 1932–35. First, the chartered banks were not firmly committed to the 10 per cent convention in the earlier period, as evidenced by the consistent tendency for the actual reserve ratio to fall below that level. By the time that the Bank of Canada went into operation, the convention had become firmly established, and the actual ratio fell below 10 per cent only occasionally between then and 1954. Second, the practice of window dressing contributed roughly 40 per cent of the difference between the ratios for the 1927–32 and 1953–58 periods. The abandonment of this practice was associated with the expiration of the Finance Act in 1935 and the fact that the Bank of Canada required the chartered banks

---

tain a 15 per cent ratio of "liquid assets" (cash reserves and short-term government securities) to deposits, in addition to the 8 per cent cash ratio discussed earlier. The effect of this measure on the desired excess *cash* position of chartered banks has apparently been slight. Fortunately, since this change applies only to the period beginning in 1955, it has no effect on the answers we are seeking with respect to bank behavior in the 1930's.

[16] Mention should be made of the chartered bank notes, which were liabilities of the chartered banks until the liability was assumed by the Bank of Canada on January 1, 1950. Prior to enactment of the Bank of Canada Act in 1935, chartered bank notes were a substantial part of the Canadian stock of currency, but have been in process of retirement since then, in accordance with the provisions of the act. Chartered banks were empowered to issue notes in amount equal to and, during the crop moving season, 15 per cent greater than their paid-in capital, upon deposit of a 5 per cent redemption fund with the Minister of Finance. The Bank Act of 1913 permitted banks to issue additional notes in any amount, but only if fully covered by deposit of gold or Dominion Notes in the Central Gold Reserve. See McIvor, *op. cit.*, pp. 83, 84, 154.

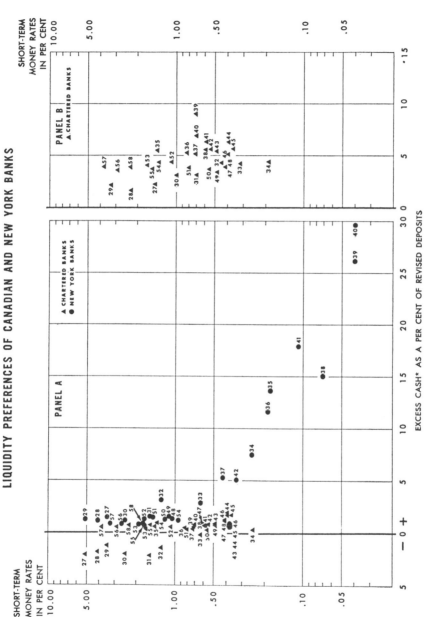

LIQUIDITY PREFERENCES OF CANADIAN AND NEW YORK BANKS

FIG. 6

*FOR DEFINITIONS OF EXCESS CASH, SEE TABLE 3.

EXCESS CASH* AS A PER CENT OF REVISED DEPOSITS

69

TABLE 3

LIQUIDITY PREFERENCES OF CANADIAN AND NEW YORK BANKS, 1927–58

CHARTERED BANK CASH ASSETS AND DEPOSIT LIABILITIES[a]
(millions of dollars)

YEAR	Cash Reserves[b]	Window Dressing[c]	Required Reserves[d]	Excess Cash Reserves[e]	Balances Due from Foreign Banks (Elsewhere)[f]	Revised Deposits[g]
	(1)	(2)	(3)	(4)	(5)	(6)
1927.......	187	8	209	−22	62	1,765
1928.......	188	17	225	−37	68	1,926
1929.......	186	26	229	−43	86	2,009
1930.......	176	21	214	−38	94	1,846
1931.......	170	12	210	−40	98	1,833
1932.......	172	14	196	−24	98	1,708
1933.......	190	5	194	− 4	76	1,684
1934.......	203	....	197	6	68	1,682
1935.......	219	....	208	11	87	1,805
1936.......	230	....	221	9	92	1,918
1937.......	244	....	236	8	97	2,054
1938.......	257	....	241	16	102	2,108
1939.......	273	....	258	15	190	2,277
1940.......	292	....	272	20	147	2,411
1941.......	315	....	298	17	150	2,636
1942.......	347	....	326	21	140	2,903
1943.......	420	....	390	30	157	3,497
1944.......	536	....	458	78	181	4,117
1945.......	602	....	528	74	192	4,727
1946.......	684	....	592	92	176	5,249
1947.......	676	....	621	55	159	5,454
1948.......	716	....	655	61	164	5,757
1949.......	760	....	718	42	166	6,251
1950.......	768	....	749	19	222	6,508
1951.......	798	....	776	22	238	6,629
1952.......	849	....	811	38	259	6,851
1953.......	884	....	862	22	269	7,235
1954.......	877	....	805	72	251	7,667
1955.......	860	....	793	67	253	8,518
1956.......	896	....	842	54	270	8,947
1957.......	896	....	848	48	311	9,017
1958.......	981	....	916	65	327	9,983

a Sources: Canada, Bank of Canada, *Statistical Summary*, Financial Supplement (Ottawa: Bank of Canada, 1946 and later years); Canada, *The Canada Gazette*, *Supplement* (Ottawa: The King's Printer, January, 1927–December, 1958); Canada, Dominion Bureau of Statistics, *Canadian Statistical Review*, 1959 *Supplement* (Ottawa: The Queen's Printer, 1959); Canada, Royal Commission on Banking and Currency in Canada, *Report* (Ottawa: The King's Printer, 1933); Stanley E. Nixon, "Interest Rates in Canada. I. The Course of Interest Rates, 1929–1937," *Canadian Journal of Economics and Political Science*, III (1937), 427–29; U.S., Board of Governors of the Federal Reserve System, *Banking and Monetary Statistics* (Washington: Board of Governors, 1943); U.S., Board of Governors of the Federal Reserve System, *Federal Reserve Bulletin* (Washington: Board of Governors, February, 1942–March, 1959) and "*J.7*" *Press Releases*, 1956–58; U.S., Bureau of the Census, *Historical Statistics of the United States* (Washington: U.S. Government Printing Office, 1960). Except where otherwise indicated, data referring to chartered bank assets and liabilities are annual averages of month-end figures taken from *The Canada Gazette*.

b Cash reserves include deposits with, and notes of, the Bank of Canada, plus subsidiary coin held by chartered banks in Canada. Prior to March, 1935, cash reserves include gold and coin in Canada, Dominion Notes, and "free" Central Gold Reserve deposits (i.e., deposits in excess of reserves against covered bank note circulation) as reported in *Statistical Summary, Financial Supplement* (1954), pp. 23–24. Cash reserves exclude window dressing in the years 1927–33. Beginning in January, 1954, data are annual averages of last Wednesday figures for each month, as reported in *Statistical Summary, Financial Supplements* (1954–58). Month-end cash tends to be lower than daily average cash beginning in 1953. This is not true for last Wednesday figures, however. The first full year for which the Wednesday data are available is 1954. Subsidiary coin in Canada, a small and relatively stable item, is derived from month-end data throughout.

c Window dressing is calculated as the difference between month-end advances to chartered banks under the Finance Act and the daily average amount of such advances, as reported in Royal Commission *Report*, *op. cit.*, p. 43. No figures for daily average advances are available for months after July, 1933. The average amount of window dressing for 1933 is based on reported figures for the first seven months of 1933.

d Required reserves are estimated to be 10 per cent of daily average "Canadian deposits" before 1946 (month end before 1935) and 10 per cent of daily average "Canadian dollar deposit liabilities" from 1946 to June, 1954. After June, 1954, required reserves are calculated as 8 per cent of Canadian dollar deposit liabilities for the average of the four Wednesdays ending with the second to the last Wednesday of the preceding month. "Canadian deposits" are from *Statistical Summary, Supplement* (1946) p. 8, and "Canadian dollar deposit liabilities" are from *Statistical Summary, Financial Supplement* (1958), p. 16.

TABLE 3—*Continued*

YEAR	CHARTERED BANK CASH ASSETS (per cent of revised dep.) Column (4) as % of (6) (7)	Columns (4)+(5) as % of (6) (8)	EXCESS CASH AS A PERCENT OF REVISED DEPOSITS N.Y. BANKS[h] (9)	SHORT-TERM MONEY RATE, CANADA[i] (10)	SHORT-TERM MONEY RATE, NEW YORK[j] (11)	NET SHORT-TERM MONEY RATE, CHARTERED BANKS[k] (12)
1927......	−1.25%	2.27%	1.42%	3.45%	3.45%	1.46%
1928......	−1.92	1.61	1.13	4.09	4.09	2.26
1929......	−2.14	2.14	1.26	5.03	5.03	3.18
1930......	−2.06	3.03	1.14	2.48	2.48	1.00
1931......	−2.18	3.16	1.52	1.57	1.57	0.70
1932......	−1.41	4.33	3.10	1.28	1.28	0.46
1933......	−0.24	4.28	2.83	0.63	0.63	0.31
1934......	0.36	4.40	7.48	0.25	0.25	0.19
1935......	0.61	5.43	13.63	1.42	0.18	1.40
1936......	0.47	5.27	11.60	0.84	0.19	0.83
1937......	0.39	5.11	5.26	0.72	0.43	0.71
1938......	0.76	5.60	15.01	0.59	0.07	0.59
1939......	0.66	9.00	26.17	0.71	0.04	0.71
1940......	0.83	6.93	29.60	0.70	0.04	0.70
1941......	0.64	6.34	17.90	0.58	0.11	0.58
1942......	0.72	5.55	5.02	0.54	0.34	0.54
1943......	0.86	5.35	0.83	0.48	0.38	0.48
1944......	1.89	6.29	0.51	0.39	0.38	0.39
1945......	1.57	5.63	0.46	0.36	0.38	0.36
1946......	1.75	5.11	0.48	0.39	0.38	0.39
1947......	1.01	3.92	0.81	0.41	0.61	0.41
1948......	1.06	3.91	1.37	0.41	1.05	0.41
1949......	0.67	3.33	1.55	0.48	1.11	0.48
1950......	0.29	3.70	1.17	0.55	1.20	0.55
1951......	0.33	3.92	1.43	0.80	1.49	0.80
1952......	0.55	4.34	1.26	1.08	1.72	1.08
1953......	0.30	4.02	0.88	1.69	1.90	1.69
1954......	0.92	4.37	1.25	1.36	0.94	1.36
1955......	0.79	3.76	0.70	1.56	1.73	1.56
1956......	0.60	3.63	0.81	2.90	2.62	2.90
1957......	0.53	3.98	0.80	3.78	3.23	3.78
1958......	0.65	3.93	0.82	2.29	1.78	2.29

e Column (1) less column (3).

f "Elsewhere" denotes balances due from foreign banks elsewhere than the U.K. The bulk of such balances are held with New York banks. After June, 1954, balances due from foreign banks elsewhere are estimated at 91.34 per cent of "deposits with other banks in non-Canadian currency," the same proportion as "elsewhere" balances bore to total balances with foreign banks in the first half of 1954.

g Sum of demand, notice, Dominion, Provincial, and foreign bank deposits, less required reserves and notes and checks of other banks. Does not include balances due to other chartered banks. Beginning in January, 1954, demand, notice, Dominion, and Provincial deposits are annual averages of last Wednesdays of each month (reported by the Bank of Canada as "Canadian dollar deposits") less month-end deposits of "other banks."

h Excess cash includes excess reserves and vault cash. Revised deposits are net demand deposits subject to reserve plus time deposits less required reserves. For 1927–55, data are averages of Wednesday figures for weekly reporting banks in New York City as reported in *Banking and Monetary Statistics*, pp. 172–95, and *Federal Reserve Bulletins*. For 1956–58, data are averages of daily figures for Central Reserve City banks in New York City (except for vault cash, where New York weekly reporting bank figures were used) as reported in "*J.7*" *Press Releases*.

i For 1927–34, represents the annual average interest rate on prime bankers' acceptances, 90 days, New York City, as reported in *Historical Statistics of the United States*, p. 654. For 1935–58, represents the annual average rate on three-month Canadian Treasury bills, as reported in Nixon, *loc. cit.*, for 1935, and in *Canadian Statistical Review*, *Supplement* (1959), p. 3, for 1936–58.

j For 1927–34, same as short-term money rate, Canada. For 1935–58, represents the annual average rate on three month U.S. Treasury bills, as reported in *Banking and Monetary Statistics*, p. 460 (dealers' quotations), 1935–41, and in *Historical Statistics*, p. 654, 1942–57, and in *Federal Reserve Bulletin* (October, 1959), p. 1276 (market yield). The yield on Treasury bills has been adjusted to a taxable equivalent basis for years 1935–41. For a description of the adjustment procedure see *infra*, p. 136.

k Net short-term money rate, Canada, less interest rate paid on inter-bank deposits, New York Federal Reserve District member banks. Interest rate paid on interbank deposits was calculated by dividing total annual interest paid on interbank deposits, from earnings statements of New York District banks as reported in *Federal Reserve Bulletins*, 1928–38, by average inter-bank deposits for the same banks as reported in *Banking and Monetary Statistics*, pp. 709, 711. Deposits were averages of figures reported for Spring and Fall call dates except in the years 1932, 1933, 1936, and 1937, when it was necessary to substitute averages of mid-year and year-end call report figures for either the Spring or Fall call dates in computing the yearly average deposits.

to report figures on a daily average basis.[17] Third, the prohibition in 1933 of payment of interest on demand deposits by U.S. banks induced Canadian banks to hold more of their cash assets in Canada and less in the form of balances with New York banks.

For these reasons, most of the increase in the excess reserve ratio of Canadian banks between 1927–35 is unquestionably the result of a shift of the preference schedule rather than a movement along it. To get an accurate impression of the slope of the schedule, it is better to confine ourselves to the observations from 1934 or 1935 through 1958. When this is done, the chart reveals little tendency for the chartered banks to accumulate excess reserves at low interest rates.[18] If so, it suggests that chartered banks behaved differently than New York City banks in the 1930's because Canadian short-term interest rates did not fall to the extremely low levels experienced in the United States. By this line of reasoning, the liquidity preference scatters of New York and Canadian banks, which tend to coincide at high interest rates (Figure 5), should have approximately the same tendency to coincide at low interest rates. This is, in fact, the case if we ignore the observations for New York banks beginning with 1932 and ending with 1942. But, of course, in so doing, we would fail to explain the very years that are of primary interest. It is clear that a liquidity trap explanation cannot account for the abnormally large

[17] Plumptre, *op. cit.*, p. 239.

[18] The observation for 1934 may be out of place, owing to possible incorrect choice of an interest rate to reflect the "cost of holding reserves" in that year. In contrast to a yield of 0.25 per cent on prime 60–90-day bankers' acceptances, the yield on 74–90-day Canadian Treasury bills averaged 2.58 per cent in 1934. We chose the acceptances yield as more representative because it is likely that the Canadian bill in 1934 lacked the high degree of liquidity it later acquired upon advent of the Bank of Canada in 1935.

Also, the observations for 1944–46 might be interpreted as showing the beginnings of a low interest rate liquidity trap. Three possible explanations for the 1944–46 observations are worth considering. One is that chartered banks expected interest rates to rise upon the war's termination, this expectation being predicated on lack of confidence in the ability or desire of the Bank of Canada to continue its low interest rate policy. A second possibility is that wartime foreign exchange controls forced chartered banks to hold a higher proportion of their cash reserves in Canada than would otherwise have been the case. The third possibility is that chartered banks held a somewhat higher cash ratio in anticipation of a revaluation of the Canadian dollar to the prewar parity. The belief was strong in Canadian financial circles that the Canadian dollar was undervalued, inasmuch as Canada had been accumulating dollar balances since early 1944, thanks to a heavy capital inflow. This revaluation occurred in July, 1946, and the cash ratio of chartered banks declined very noticeably in the remainder of that year. See McIvor, *op. cit.*, pp. 165–235, and B. H. Higgins, *Canada's Financial System in War*, Occasional Paper 19 (New York: National Bureau of Economic Research, 1944), pp. 33–35. Also see P. M. Cornell, "Exchange Flexibility in Canada: Some Underlying Factors," *Public Policy* (Cambridge, Mass.: Graduate School of Public Administration, Harvard University, 1958), VIII, 271.

excess cash ratios of New York banks in the years 1932–34, 1937, and 1942, at levels of interest rates comparable with those experienced by Canadian banks. And it is equally clear that, when the scatters for New York and chartered banks do coincide, there is no evidence of the presence of a liquidity trap for either set of banks. At best, the trap hypothesis has some measure of plausibility only for 1939 and 1940, years when the U.S. Treasury bill rate was substantially lower than the lowest bill rates ever attained in Canada (or any other country, for that matter).[19]

One objection to this analysis is that the reserve position of chartered banks may have been defined too narrowly, for they characteristically hold large balances on deposit with banks outside Canada, principally in New York. To meet this point, a scatter diagram of the ratio of the sum of excess cash in Canada plus deposits with New York banks to revised deposits plotted against the short-term interest rate for Canadian banks (less the interest rate paid on inter-bank balances by banks in the New York Federal Reserve District) is presented in panel B of Figure 6. Once again, the chartered banks give no evidence of developing a liquidity trap condition at low interest rates. In one year, 1939, the ratio did indeed reach the unusually high level of 9 per cent. The Canadian dollar however, was devalued by 10 per cent relative to the U.S. dollar in September of that year. The rapid increase in chartered bank balances due from New York banks in the ten months preceding devaluation, and the almost equally sharp decline of these balances in the ensuing months, supports the view that the devaluation was anticipated and that the chartered banks were attempting to profit from it by accumulating foreign exchange assets.

It seems fair to conclude, then, that Canadian banks, with the qualifications noted earlier, give the appearance of moving along a stable liq-

---

[19] It should be noted that our choice of the Canadian Treasury bill rate as a measure of the cost of holding excess cash for chartered banks (after 1934) affords the best possible comparison from the standpoint of the liquidity trap hypothesis. It can be argued, for example, that the relevant interest rates for this purpose are not Canadian short-term rates but U.S. rates, for several reasons—the close proximity of the administrative offices of the Canadian banks to New York, the absence of an organized money market in Canada until recent years, the close commercial and financial ties between the two countries, plus the fact that the chartered banks carry considerable balances with New York banks and continue to invest in U.S. short-term money market claims. Accordingly, if we compared excess cash ratios of the two sets of banks, each plotted against, say, the U.S. Treasury bill rate, call loan rate, or commercial paper rate, the contrast between the performances of Canadian and New York banks in the 1930's would be even more pronounced, since none of the aforementioned divergences in cash ratios would appear to have been caused by differences in levels of interest rates. An important weakness in this argument, however, is that it neglects forward exchange transactions (see *supra* p. 67).

uidity preference schedule throughout the period from 1935–58, and that this schedule shows no appreciable tendency to flatten out at low interest rates.

How can the differences between U.S. and Canadian bank behavior in the 1930's be explained? We have seen that disparities in interest rate levels can explain only part of the difference. Nor can expectations of future interest rates be an important factor, since there is little reason to think that expectations of Canadian and U.S. bankers differed systematically in that respect. Again, declines in real and money income to 1933 and their subsequent recoveries were sufficiently alike in the two countries as to rule out factors related to demand for credit by the public from playing a crucial role.

With only a handful of banks to deal with, it might be thought that the possibilities for exercise of moral suasion by banking authorities were greater in Canada and that in the interests of promoting economic recovery pressure may have been exerted on the chartered banks to restrain them from excessive accumulation of cash in the 1930's. In support of this proposition, one can point to the action of the government in forcing the banks to borrow $35 million of Dominion Notes in November, 1932, at 3 per cent interest. This program was carried out under the provisions of the Finance Act and involved a simultaneous purchase by the banks of an equal amount of 4 per cent Treasury bills having a maturity of two years, the bills being used as collateral for the Finance Act borrowing. Although the banks were prohibited from repaying the $35 million for two years, the experiment went largely for naught, because it merely accelerated the repayment by the banks of their previous borrowings under the Finance Act.[20] Aside from this episode, there is no evidence that moral suasion was attempted in Canada during the decade. According to Neufeld: "It is clear that up to early 1939 the moral suasion of the Bank [of Canada] had not been really tested, that by itself it probably could not have stood a determined test, and that more time and different economic conditions were required for further development."[21]

Another possibility, and one which seems to offer a better clue to the reasons for the contrast in the behavior of Canadian and U.S. banks, is that during the 1930's the absence of runs on banks, bank failures, and drastic revisions in reserve requirements allowed Canadian banks to operate in an atmosphere of comparative confidence and safety despite serious economic depression.

Public confidence in the Canadian banking system was undoubtedly

[20] McIvor, *op. cit.*, p. 133.   [21] Neufeld, *op. cit.*, p. 76.

engendered by the nature of branch banking, which can mobilize cash resources to meet a localized run on deposits more effectively than can a
unit banking setup. It is interesting to note that the only comparable
branch bank in the United States in the 1930's, the Bank of America,
easily withstood runs and by the end of the decade, at least, held quite
negligible excess reserves as a percentage of its deposit liabilities.[22] But
even if we conclude from this that branch banks are relatively immune to
the ravages of bank panics, it is clear that unit banks are not and that this
difference shows up in the contrast between the cash positions of Canadian
and U.S. banks in the years following the 1933 bank holiday.

S.R. Noble, former assistant general manager of the Bank of Canada,
expressed this view very well in 1937:

The conditions in Canada provided a better laboratory to conduct financial
experiments than, for example, the United States provides. In the latter country
the public exhibited a lack of confidence in the banking system which finally
became complete with the crisis of March 1933, and hoarding of currency took
place on a scale unprecedented in any country. A similar phenomenon did not
occur in Canada and the standing of Canadian banking institutions was never
questioned. Monetary actions can be expected to give prompt results only when
the commercial banking machinery is operating normally. . . . As soon as the
banks were provided with surplus reserves by the change in the Dominion Notes
Act of June 28, 1934 [which increased the volume of Dominion Notes very sub-
stantially], deposits immediately began to grow and have continued to do so up
to the present time.[23]

This passage suggests that it was not differences between the two countries in rates of growth in bank reserves but differences in the way banks
responded to this growth which really account for the different patterns
of cash holdings. A more rapid expansion in reserves in the U.S. relative
to Canada undoubtedly led to some of the disparity in the excess reserve
ratios of the two banking systems in the 1930's. Between 1933–39,
chartered bank cash plus foreign bank balances increased by an average of
11.7 per cent per year, whereas the corresponding figure for all U.S.
member banks[24] was 16.5 per cent, and, for weekly reporting banks in

[22] The call reports of the Bank of America show excess reserves plus vault cash
amounted to −0.2 per cent of revised deposits on December 31, 1939, and 2.6 per cent
on December 31, 1940. Excess reserves calculated from call reports are only approximate, of course.

[23] S. R. Noble, "The Monetary Experience of Canada during the Depression," in
A. D. Gayer (ed.), *The Lessons of Monetary Experience* (New York: Farrar & Rinehart,
1937), p. 127.

[24] The relevant comparison for the U.S. is deposit-creating potential, i.e., total reserves divided by the average required reserve ratio so as to allow for changes in reserve
requirements.

New York, it was 35.0 per cent. The rise, however, in the excess reserve ratios of New York banks relative to those of the chartered banks would seem to be far out of proportion to the differences in the rates of increase in total reserves for the two groups of banks. The banks by their own actions must have made the biggest contribution to the divergence in excess reserve ratios.

Moreover, the differences in rates of growth of total reserves of chartered and New York banks were in part a result of, not a cause of, differences in the willingness of the two sets of banks to expand loans and deposits on the basis of given additions to total reserves. If Canadian banks had been supplied additional reserves at a rate equal to the growth of potential deposits in the U.S. banking system, Canadian banks would have then created deposits at a faster rate of growth and Canada might have experienced more rapid advances in real income and prices than it did. We have seen that rates of increase in real and money income were roughly of the same magnitude in Canada and the United States between 1933–40. The reason why reserves were not supplied at a faster rate is that the monetary authorities were attempting to maintain an approximately fixed exchange rate against the U.S. dollar.[25] Their success is shown by the fact that between January, 1935, and August, 1939, the Canadian–U.S. exchange rate, although supposedly a floating one, remained nearly constant.[26] To have encouraged the Canadian economy to advance more rapidly by monetary-fiscal means might well have necessitated the abandonment of the fixed exchange rate, inasmuch as higher Canadian prices and incomes and possibly lower interest rates would all have tended to create a deficit in the Canadian balance of payments.

The dissimilar response of Canadian and New York banks to increased bank reserves may be attributed to either the "shock" effect or the "inertia" effect as outlined in the previous chapter. Either New York banks suddenly, out of shock, wanted to hold much greater amounts of excess reserves or, perhaps equally suddenly, lost confidence in the permanence

[25] The Bank of Canada refused to take credit for stabilizing the exchange rate during this period despite allegations in the financial press that this was, in fact, its policy. See "Central Bank Credited for Exchange Stability," *Financial Post* (Toronto), October 29, 1938, p. 11; and Banking Supplements, *Economist* (London), October 17, 1936, p. 13; October 16, 1937, p. 12; and October 29, 1938, p. 14. Also see the statement of Graham Towers, Governor of the Bank of Canada, reprinted in I. Brecher, *Monetary and Fiscal Thought and Policy in Canada, 1919–39* (Toronto: University of Toronto Press, 1957), p. 314.

[26] In 1933–34, the U.S. dollar varied from $0.835 to $1.029 per Canadian dollar. But between January, 1935, and August, 1939, the range was only from $0.986 to $1.002. See U.S., Board of Governors of the Federal Reserve System, *Banking and Monetary Statistics* (Washington: Board of Governors, 1943), p. 665.

of their existing deposit-creating potential. Both possibilities suggest that it is New York banks, not Canadian banks whose behavior is to be considered unusual during the 1930's. The shock explanation must seek evidence that New York banks did, in fact, raise their desired excess reserve positions because of recurring liquidity crises. The inertia or transitory potential deposits hypothesis would have to demonstrate that during the 1930's New York banks reacted with a longer expectational lag to changes in reserves and reserve requirements than in previous or subsequent periods. Also, if one or the other of these explanations is correct, it should be possible to discern the same effect after other bank panics in U.S. history. These issues are examined in detail, beginning in Chapter VI.

But in any case, shock and inertia are only manifestations of the underlying traumatic circumstances of U.S. banking in the 1930's. The fact that the Canadian banking environment of these years was, by comparison, relatively tranquil, goes a long way toward accounting for the extreme contrast between the cash positions of Canadian and U.S. banks during the Great Depression.

A more thoroughgoing study of Canadian banking would in all probability resolve some of the minor puzzles in the data, arrive at a more precise definition and measurement of the excess cash position of the chartered banks, make allowances for the effects of fluctuations in exchange rates on the value in Canadian currency, of foreign balances, and intensively examine the influence of forward exchange rates on the banks' cash positions. But for the issue of major interest here—the comparative liquidity preferences of U.S. and Canadian banks in the face of low and declining interest rates during the 1930's—the results are not likely to be altered significantly.

VI

New York Clearing House Banks, 1872–1914

THE BANKING CRISIS of the early 1930's was only the latest of a series of episodes in which external or internal drains of high-powered money gave rise to bank panics and severe financial distress. The national banking era,[1] from 1863–1914, contained four notable banking crises—September, 1873; May, 1884; August, 1893; and October, 1907—and two of the most serious depressions in U.S. history—1873–79 and 1893–97. Examination of this period should therefore provide additional evidence to test hypotheses developed to explain the banking experience of the 1930's.

A well-known feature of the banking system in this era was the tendency for banking reserves to be shifted into and out of central reserve city banks, particularly those in New York, as fluctuations in demands for currency and loan funds altered the relative returns that interior banks could earn on those reserves in their own localities relative to the interest they received on deposits with reserve agents.

---

[1] The legal framework of the pre–Federal Reserve national banking system can be summarized briefly. Under the National Bank Acts of 1863 and 1864, a national bank was empowered to issue national bank notes to the extent of 90 per cent (100 per cent after 1900) of the par or market value (whichever was less) of certain U.S. government bonds bearing the "circulation privilege" when these bonds were deposited by the bank with the U.S. Treasury. Notes could be issued in amount not exceeding 90 per cent of the bank's capital (100 per cent after 1900). Until 1874, the required lawful money reserve against both national bank notes and net deposit liabilities of national banks was 15 per cent for country banks and 25 per cent for reserve city and central reserve city banks. Up to three-fifths of the required reserves of country banks could take the form of deposits with "reserve agent" banks in reserve and central reserve cities, and one-half of the required reserves of reserve city banks could be deposited with reserve agents in central reserve cities. Central reserve city banks were required to keep the full 25 per cent requirement in the form of vault reserves of lawful money (which included specie and legal tender notes but not national bank notes). National banks were required to keep reserves up to the legal minimum at all times. Failure to do so made it illegal for a bank to incur additional liabilities except sight drafts, and opened the way to receivership. After June 20, 1874, the reserve requirement against national bank notes was replaced by the requirement to hold a 5 per cent lawful money redemption fund on deposit with the Treasury against outstanding notes. However, the redemption fund could be counted as part of reserves against net deposits. Net deposits were defined as gross deposits less: exchanges for clearing houses, checks on other banks in the same city, notes of other than national banks, and balances due from other banks up to an amount not to exceed balances due to other banks. After May 30, 1908, gross deposits excluded Treasury deposits, for purposes of required reserve calculations.

78

The pooling of reserves in New York placed a burden on that money market to develop procedures for adjusting to fluctuations in demands for cash by interior banks and by the non-bank public. The vulnerability of New York banks to cash drains was compounded by "inelasticity" of the nation's currency stock in the face of shifts in the demand for currency relative to deposits. Greenbacks and the various forms of currency arising from silver purchase programs were issued in amounts or at rates that were fixed by law, with no provision for emergency expansion or contraction. The national bank note circulation failed to provide the necessary elasticity because of various delays involved in the process of obtaining new notes from the Treasury.[2]

New York banks characteristically carried very small amounts of excess cash reserves. Under most circumstances, cash drains could be met by liquidating call loans and other short-term bank assets. In the process, interest rates in the New York money market tended to rise and stock prices tended to decline, thereby inducing foreign and domestic investors to send funds to the New York money market and thus counteract the drain. In years of extreme pressure, when liquidation of loans proved ineffective, New York Clearing House Banks agreed to accept clearing house loan certificates in lieu of cash settlement of net clearing house balances. Banks with net deficits borrowed from the clearing house, pledging collateral in return for loan certificates. In effect, strong banks lent reserves to weak banks. This procedure was successful in relieving pressure only when it was confined to a few banks.[3]

When these methods failed to halt a bank panic, the New York banks restricted convertibility of deposits into currency. This drastic measure helped bring an end to the crises of 1873, 1893, and 1907. In the 1907 panic, restriction of cash payments was extremely widespread throughout the nation and was aided by the issuance of clearing house certificates in currency denominations for hand-to-hand circulation.[4] Currency went to a premium in relation to bank deposits and rates of exchange of in-town for out-of-town bank drafts fluctuated widely. Presumably the certificates of a given clearing house were also exchangeable for legal tender at a fluctuating discount and for certificates of other clearing houses at fluctuating exchange rates.

[2] M. G. Myers, *The New York Money Market, Origins and Development* (New York: Columbia University Press, 1931), p. 405.

[3] See O. M. W. Sprague, *History of Crises under the National Banking System*, National Monetary Commission (Washington: U.S. Government Printing Office, 1910), p. 182.

[4] See A. P. Andrews, "Substitutes for Cash in the Panic of 1907," *Quarterly Journal of Economics*, XXII (August, 1908), 497–516.

Restriction of cash payment served the purpose of forestalling a continuation of the vicious circle of runs on banks, bank failures, and still more runs on banks. The restriction of cash payments allowed a breathing spell until the outflow of currency from banks could be reversed. This reversal was brought about by a number of forces—slackening of panic hysteria, gold inflows from abroad,[5] reduced demand for currency engendered by the business depression that frequently accompanied panics, transfer of Treasury cash balances to banks, and seasonal factors. Eventually, the premium on cash over deposits or "script" would narrow to the point where restriction of cash payments could be lifted.

With the aid of weekly data on movements of cash into and out of New York Clearing House Banks, as published in the *Commercial and Financial Chronicle*, it is possible to be somewhat more specific.

The 1884 panic was relatively localized in its initial impact. Almost the sole sources of cash drains were intra-city losses—to the public and to non–Clearing House New York Banks. The accumulation of reserves in the year following the May crisis date was due to net inflows of gold, transfers of funds from the subtreasury, and remittances from the "interior" (the rest of the United States), in roughly equal amounts. Intra-city losses continued, but at a slackened pace.

The panics of 1893 and 1907 were similar in their respective patterns of cash flows, but these differed from the 1884 pattern in that cash drains in the period of actual panic consisted not only of intra-city losses, but of large withdrawals of funds by the interior as well. Indeed, the variations in the Clearing House Banks' reserves in the year following the 1893 and the 1907 crisis dates were strongly dominated by movements of cash to and from the interior. Gold inflows commenced soon after the onset of these crises, but within one or two months, the accretion from this source had virtually ceased. Toward the end of the first year after each of these crises, gold flows reversed themselves, while total reserves continued to mount. Subtreasury operations added to bank reserves in a pattern rather similar to gold flows, except for one difference: the contribution of subtreasury operations was somewhat smaller in amount, on average. In 1907 the subtreasury moved more quickly than in 1893 to bolster the cash positions

---

[5] Friedman and Schwartz suggest two reasons for the gold inflow: (a) Depreciation of the deposit dollar in terms of gold or foreign exchange was expected to be temporary. This led to speculative conversion of gold into deposit dollars. (b) The premium on currency relative to deposits created an arbitrage incentive to import gold that was not quickly removed by a rise in the price of gold and foreign exchange in terms of deposits. M. Friedman and A. Schwartz, *A Monetary History of the United States, 1867–1960* (Princeton, N.J.: Princeton University Press for the National Bureau of Economic Research, 1963), pp. 110, 161–62.

of New York banks and withdrew funds less abruptly after the crisis had passed.

EXCESS RESERVES OF NEW YORK BANKS

Following each serious banking crisis, the excess cash reserve ratio of New York Clearing House Banks mounted rapidly to a peak, then declined somewhat more gradually to normal levels, which were generally only slightly in excess of reserve requirements (Figure 7). After 1873, excess cash remained at rather high levels until 1879, while after 1884 and 1893, the excess cash ratio rose rapidly to a peak, then fell almost as rapidly. The peak came about one year after the crisis in 1884 and about five months after the crisis in 1893. It is important to note that the buildup in the excess cash reserve ratio of New York banks was quite moderate and brief following the 1907 crisis.[6] In addition, there are other years in which milder increases in the cash positions of New York banks occurred, notably 1890–92, 1896–97, and 1903–4. Financial disturbances were associated with each of these periods: minor bank panics in 1890 and 1903 and a speculative flight from the dollar in 1896. Apart from the cyclical fluctuations in the excess cash reserve ratio, a slight downtrend in the ratio can be discerned by comparison of successive non-crisis periods.

The tendency, during the national banking period for the excess cash reserve ratio to reach unusual heights after liquidity crises, bears a similarity to the pattern of fluctuation in excess cash of U.S. banks during the 1930's and suggests that an explanation may exist in terms of factors common to all banking crises.[7] In the remainder of this chapter and in the

[6] A similar, though less pronounced pattern of postpanic fluctuation in the excess cash reserve positions of reserve city and country national banks can also be observed. See Myers, *op. cit.*, p. 236. In contrast with the New York banks' pattern, postpanic excess reserve ratios of other (interior) banks were greatest after the 1907 panic and least after the 1884 panic. Our analysis will be confined to New York Clearing House Banks. The availability of weekly and monthly data for these banks, compared with the irregularly spaced call reports for national banks, simplifies seasonal adjustment procedures and makes it possible to follow crisis developments more precisely. Moreover, the lack of time series data for interest paid on correspondent bank balances hampers estimation of the net cost of holding excess reserves for reserve city and country banks. New York banks, on the other hand, held negligible correspondent bank balances, so the problem does not arise in the analysis of their excess reserve position. It should be noted that the excess cash reserve ratio for New York Clearing House Banks is calculated as the ratio of excess reserves of lawful money to "revised deposits" (i.e., net deposits subject to reserve less required reserves).

[7] Banking crises also plagued British banking in the nineteenth and early twentieth centuries. In the space of sixty years, the London money market suffered five bank panics—in October, 1847; November, 1857; May, 1866; May, 1875; and November, 1890—while October was a month of very severe pressure in 1877, 1878, and 1907. An analysis

[Footnote continued on page 83]

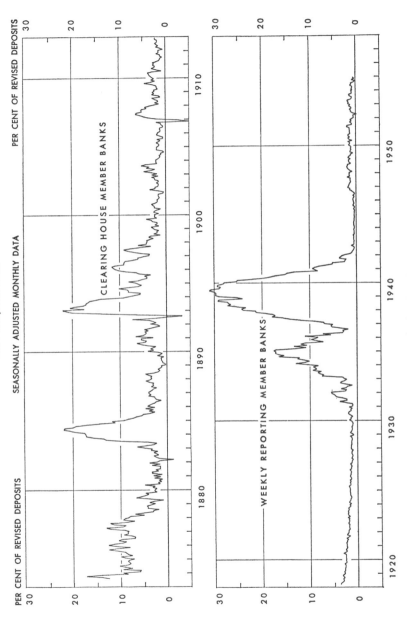

EXCESS CASH RESERVE RATIO OF NEW YORK BANKS
1874-1913, 1919-1955

SEASONALLY ADJUSTED MONTHLY DATA

PER CENT OF REVISED DEPOSITS

PER CENT OF REVISED DEPOSITS

CLEARING HOUSE MEMBER BANKS

WEEKLY REPORTING MEMBER BANKS

1880   1890   1900   1910

1920   1930   1940   1950

¹ EXCESS CASH INCLUDES VAULT CASH AND RESERVES IN EXCESS OF LEGAL REQUIREMENTS

Fig. 7

one to follow, a number of variables will be examined for their ability to explain variations in the excess cash ratio of New York banks, both during the national banking period and in the period since the founding of the Federal Reserve System. These variables will include the following: cost of holding excess cash, rate of bank failure, business failure liabilities, time elapsed since previous crisis, risk premiums on corporate bonds, transitory cash reserves, and the spread between short and long-term interest rates.

Variables to be Tested

The present chapter will confine itself to tests on annual data for the national banking period, while the following chapter will employ monthly data and cover both the national banking and Federal Reserve periods. Discussion of the last three of the variables mentioned will be deferred to the following chapter.

A. Cost of Holding Reserves

According to both the liquidity trap and "alternative" hypotheses, the level of the excess cash reserve ratio should be inversely related to the opportunity cost of holding such reserves, as measured by the return on earning assets. For New York banks, until the depression of the 1930's, the closest substitutes for cash were call loans to brokers collateralized by stocks and bonds listed on the New York Stock Exchange. Commercial paper, time loans on stocks and bonds, and bankers' acceptances were also relatively liquid and important components of bank portfolios, but

---

[Footnote continued from page 81]

of the behavior of London banks in response to these disturbances would be a suitable companion to our investigation of New York Clearing House Banks. Unfortunately, the available data do not permit such an analysis to be made. London clearing bankers' balances with the Bank of England are available for the period from 1844–77 and deposit liabilities of the London joint stock banks are also available for the same period. The joint stock banks, however, were not admitted to membership in the clearing house association until May, 1854, and the private bankers who were members did not publish their deposit figures. Also, at this time a system of settlement of accounts by transfers on the books of the Bank of England was replacing the earlier system of settlement by transfer of Bank of England notes. This resulted in a shift of reserves from vault cash to the Bank of England. With the exception of the London and Westminster Bank, the published balance sheets of London joint stock banks did not segregate cash and money lent at call or short notice. Although precise data are lacking, we have the testimony of Bagehot, Palgrave, and the bankers themselves as to a definite inclination on the part of London banks to accumulate cash after banking crises. On these points, see R. H. Palgrave, *Bank Rate and the Money Market* (London: John Murray, 1903), pp. 13, 21, 24–27; S. E. Thomas, *The Rise and Growth of Joint Stock Banking* (London: Sir Isaac Pitman & Sons, 1934), I, 547–75, 663–67; R. P. Higonnet, "Bank Deposits in the United Kingdom, 1870–1914," *Quarterly Journal of Economics*, LXXI (August, 1957), 339–44; W. Bagehot, *Lombard Street* (London: Kegan Paul and Co., 1873), pp. 57–61, 319–29.

the call loan was the preeminent debt instrument of the money market and the staple of the New York banks' secondary reserve positions.[8] Macaulay's monthly series of call money renewal rates begins in 1857, as does his series on commercial paper rates. Unfortunately, the rates on both commercial paper and call money incorporate a risk premium element, especially in the earlier years. For example, call loan rates on default free and highly marketable securities, such as government bonds and, in later years, rates on bankers' acceptances, tended to be significantly lower than call loan rates on "mixed" stock exchange collateral that form the basis of Macaulay's series.[9]

B. Bank Failures and Suspensions

A banking crisis tends to leave an imprint on bankers generally, and it would be reasonable to expect them to hold abnormally large amounts of excess cash reserves in the ensuing recovery period when the lessons of the crisis are fresh. Indeed, in a unit banking system this response may be typical of any period when the rate of bank failures or suspensions is high, since the threat of runs on other banks is then likely to be intensified.[10]

There are many ways in which one might measure financial difficulty among banks. Losses incurred by depositors or stockholders in failed or merged banks, total capital, deposits, or liabilities of suspended banks, and their size, age, and geographical distributions all may play important roles in determining the expectations of the community about the likelihood of a disruption of normal banking conditions. Unfortunately, lack of suitable data for a sufficiently long period rules out many of these measures, and even the most reliable data on bank failures have such deficiencies as to render them, at best, only rough indicators of the characteristics they purport to measure.

I decided to experiment with two series: (*a*) total deposit liabilities of national bank failures and suspensions involving either receivership or temporary administration by national bank examiners, deflated by deposits of all national banks (June call dates); and (*b*) a combined series comprising deposits of national bank failures and suspensions plus lia-

---

[8] For a description of short-term money rates and money markets in New York under the national banking system, see F. R. Macaulay, *The Movements of Interest Rates, Bond Yields and Stock Prices in the United States since 1856* (New York: National Bureau of Economic Research, 1938), pp. A335–51. Also see Myers, *op. cit.*, pp. 265–87, and B. Griffis, *The New York Call Money Market* (New York: Ronald Press, 1925), pp. 27–32.

[9] Macaulay, *op. cit.*, pp. A335–40; Myers, *op. cit.*, pp. 280–81. Also see Griffis, *op. cit.*, pp. 16–26.

[10] Except under an effective regime of deposit insurance.

bilities or resources of failed state and private banks, deflated by total bank deposits of the public and Treasury.

C. Business Failures

A more general indicator of economic distress is provided by figures on liabilities of business failures. In a period of high business failure rates, defaults on loans should also increase, and one might expect banks to revise upward their allowances for bad debts.[11] For a given gross interest return on loans, this would, of course, imply a lowering of the expected net return from new loans or extensions of existing loans. Thus liabilities of business failures may act as a proxy for an index of the risk premium on loans. To the extent that the available short-term interest rate may incorporate a risk component, such an index might offer a means for separating the effect of the "pure" interest component from the risk component.

In tests reported below, the Dun and Bradstreet series of failure liabilities of commercial and industrial enterprises is used, deflated by net national product in current dollars. This series is not entirely satisfactory as an indicator of lending risks of banks inasmuch as it excludes liabilities of failures in finance, insurance, real estate, railroads, farming, and many types of professional, small service, and construction enterprises.

D. Time Elapsed since Previous Crisis: The Shock Effect

The banking crisis is perhaps not amenable to the usual sort of numerical representation. In most crises, there tends to be a rather clearly defined date in time when the pressure on the banks reaches such a point that normal banking procedures are suspended and emergency measures are instituted to restore order. The constellation of factors that determines when this point is reached in a given crisis tends to be different from those of any other crisis. The salient feature of all crises may be the shock itself, whatever its causes, that induces banks to take drastic remedial action to prevent further drains of reserves. If it is usually possible to specify the point in time when the crisis strain reaches this peak, it is plausible to suppose that banks desire to hold a sharply higher level of excess reserves at that time. As time passes, and provided that no serious new disturbances occur, the desired level of excess cash reserves will gradually return to normal levels. But it would be unreasonable to expect

[11] Annual gross losses per one hundred dollars of loans and investments of all national banks were, in fact, highly correlated with the annual rate of business failures during the period 1890–1931. See U.S., Federal Reserve System, Committee on Branch, Group, and Chain Banking, "Banking Profits, 1890–1931" (unpublished report by the Committee, 1933), p. 62, (mimeographed).

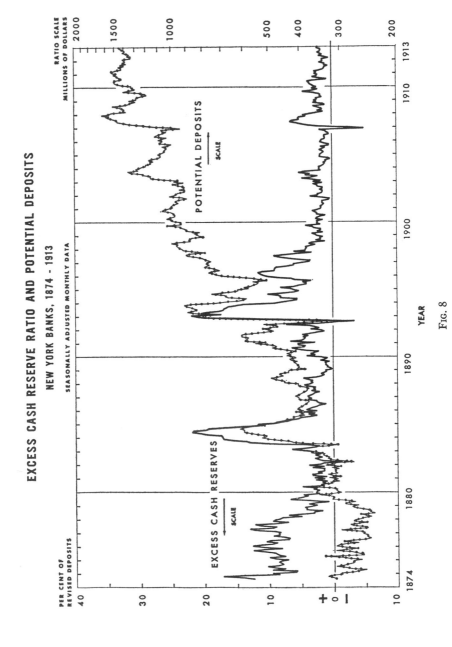

EXCESS CASH RESERVE RATIO AND POTENTIAL DEPOSITS

NEW YORK BANKS, 1874 - 1913

SEASONALLY ADJUSTED MONTHLY DATA

PER CENT OF
REVISED DEPOSITS

RATIO SCALE

MILLIONS OF DOLLARS

POTENTIAL DEPOSITS

SCALE

EXCESS CASH RESERVES

SCALE

YEAR

Fig. 8

banks as a whole to be able to attain the desired level of excess cash reserves instantaneously or shortly after a crisis date. This would require wholesale liquidation of earning assets at severe losses and would lead to bankruptcy of the institutions attempting it. Instead, we envisage an adjustment process, in which banks add to their excess reserves at a rate that is proportional to the difference between their desired and their actual level of excess reserves.

The full testing of this hypothesis will require the use of monthly data and is deferred to the following chapter. If, as in the present chapter, our data take the form of annual averages we may assume that the desired excess cash reserve ratio is approximated by the actual ratio, provided that the rate of adjustment proceeds rapidly enough. Our "crisis variable" can then be represented by time, in years after the previous crisis. Later, in dealing with monthly data, a somewhat more refined time variable will be introduced.

Statistical Tests

Table 4 presents the results of a series of regressions, fitted by least squares methods, to annual data for the period 1872–1913. In each regression, the dependent variable is ρ_t, excess cash reserves as a percentage of revised deposits for New York Clearing House Banks.

Equations (6.1) and (6.2) show short-term interest rates to be significant at the five per cent level, but only a third or less of the total variance of the excess reserve percentage is explained by interest rates alone.[12] The call loan rate is superior to the commercial paper rate as an explanatory variable, as might be expected from our previous discussion.

A moderate improvement in fit is effected by the incorporation of the all-bank failure and suspension rate in (6.3) and (6.4), but the suspension rate for national banks proved to have little explanatory power. Examination of the residuals for (6.4) disclosed that the observed excess reserve percentage consistently exceeded the predicted percentage by substantial amounts in years immediately following crises. One reason for this is that high rates of bank suspensions tend to precede bank panics,[13] whereas the

[12] For two previous statistical studies of the relation between call loan rates and the reserve position of New York Clearing House Banks, see J. P. Norton, *Statistical Studies in the New York Money Market* (New York: MacMillan Co., 1902), and L. H. Seltzer and S. L. Horner, "Bank Reserves and the Call Money Loan Rate," *Journal of Political Economy*, XXX (February, 1922), 108–18. Norton fitted what may be interpreted as liquidity preference equations, covering the period 1885–1900, while Seltzer and Horner covered the period 1901–9. Each study found a correlation coefficient of −.52 between the reserve ratio and the call loan rate.

[13] This lead, however, is reduced somewhat by the delays in appointing receivers for state banks. The reported failure dates in the case of state and private banks do not always represent the date when the bank closed its doors.

TABLE 4

REGRESSIONS, NEW YORK CLEARING HOUSE BANKS

(Annual Data)

EQUATION NUMBER	TIME PERIOD COVERED	NUMBER OF OBSERVATIONS	CONSTANT TERM	COEFFICIENTS AND STANDARD ERRORS (IN PARENTHESES) OF INDEPENDENT VARIABLES*											R^2
				r_t	$\log_e r_t$	$\log r_t$	$\log_e c_t$	S_t	S_{t-1}	N_{St}	F_t	F_{t-1}	$\log \tilde{i}$	$\log_e \tilde{i}$	
6.1	1872–1913	42	14.805				−6.226 (2.715)								.116
6.2	1872–1913	42	11.181		−4.918 (1.100)										.333
6.3	1872–1913	42	17.246				−8.580 (2.713)	2.010 (.795)							.241
6.4	1872–1913	42	10.660		−5.423 (1.039)			1.762 (.653)							.438
6.5	1872–1913	42	16.534				−7.612 (2.859)			1.414 (1.008)					.159
6.6	1872–1913	42	11.068		−5.113 (1.104)					1.035 (.834)					.359
6.7	1872–1913	42	7.824		−3.561 (1.125)				2.351 (.680)						.498
6.8	1872–1913	42	19.536				−12.502 (2.052)				4.113 (.594)				.604
6.9	1872–1913	42	13.978		−5.760 (.794)						3.115 (.492)				.671
6.10	1872–1913	42	5.422		−4.087 (.705)							3.517 (.424)			.767
6.11	1874–1909	34	23.989			−9.585 (3.243)							−5.222 (1.412)		.638
6.12	1874–1909	34	14.202			−16.712 (3.081)									.479

TABLE 4—Continued

COEFFICIENTS AND STANDARD ERRORS (IN PARENTHESES) OF INDEPENDENT VARIABLES*

EQUATION NUMBER	TIME PERIOD COVERED	NUMBER OF OBSERVATIONS	CONSTANT TERM	r_t	$\log_e r_t$	$\log r_t$	$\log_e c_t$	S_t	S_{t-1}	N_{S_t}	F_t	F_{t-1}	$\log \tilde{i}$	$\log_e \tilde{i}$	R^2
6.13	1874–1909	34	1.978	−.743 (.265)									−.377 (.116)		.594
6.14	1874–1909	34	1.271	−1.258 (.244)											.455
6.15	1872–1913	42	9.158		−4.392 (.997)						2.559 (.531)			−1.368 (.645)	.706
6.16	1872–1913	42	17.774				−8.794 (2.160)				3.112 (.614)			−1.935 (.593)	.690
6.17	1872–1913	42	11.592					1.510 (.565)						−2.606 (.676)	.596
6.18	1872–1913	42	15.754		−3.010 (1.091)		−4.472 (2.229)	1.625 (.616)						−3.246 (.616)	.561
6.19	1872–1913	42	6.466		−3.288 (.810)							3.108 (.467)		−1.033 (.562)	.787
6.20	1872–1913	42	6.650		−3.425 (.865)				.287 (.539)			3.268 (.575)		−1.051 (.569)	.788

*The dependent variable in regressions 6.1–6.20 is excess reserves as a percentage of revised deposits. Independent variables are symbolized as follows:

r_t = Call loan renewal rate, percent.

c_t = Commercial paper rate, percent.

S_t = Deposits or liabilities of bank failures or suspensions, all banks as a percentage of total deposits of Treasury and public.

N_{S_t} = Deposits of suspended national banks as a percentage of total deposits, national banks.

F_t = Liabilities of business failures as a percentage of net national product.

$\tilde{i}$ = Number of years since previous crisis date.

high levels of excess reserves always occur after the panic has passed. The lagged failure and suspension rate for all banks yielded an improvement in fit, as shown in (6.7), although only a moderate one. Prediction in the year following each crisis is improved, but a pronounced downtrend exists in the residuals (observed less predicted excess reserve percentage) for both this regression and regressions (6.3)–(6.6).

Equations (6.8) and (6.9), in which the rate of business failure liabilities replaces the rate of bank suspensions, proved to be more successful in predicting the excess reserve percentage. The residuals again tend to be large in all immediate post-crisis years except 1908, however. Since the business failure rate tends to be highest in crisis years, it seemed reasonable to experiment with F_t lagged one year, as in (6.10). This regression predicts postcrisis fluctuations in the excess reserve percentage fairly satisfactorily and eliminates virtually all of the downtrend in residuals observed in previous regressions.

The remainder of the regressions in Table 4 have as their objective the testing of special forms of the time-elapsed-from-previous crisis hypothesis. In (6.11)–(6.14), the observational time units are complete years after the previous crisis date. Thus r_t is averaged for successive twelve-month periods, beginning with the month following the previous crisis date, and $\bar{t}$ in these regressions is the average length of time for complete years following the previous crisis beginning with the month after the crisis date.[14] A comparison of residuals for (6.12) and (6.14) with those for (6.11) and (6.13), respectively, reveals that the inclusion of the logarithm of time after crisis reduces the residuals in years immediately following crises, except after the 1907 panic, when the accumulation of excess reserves was moderate. Nevertheless, the residuals in (6.11) and (6.13) again display a distinct downward trend: observed exceeds predicted in the early years and falls short of predicted in later years.

In (6.15)–(6.20), all variables are measured for calendar year time units and the period covered in these regressions is 1872–1913, whereas the previous group covered 1874–1909. The objective in these six regressions was to determine whether the addition of $\log_e \bar{t}$ effects an improvement in the fits obtained from regressions (6.3), (6.4), (6.8), (6.9), or (6.10). The results are somewhat equivocal. The new variable substantially enhances the predictive power when introduced into equations involving the all-bank suspension rate (regressions [6.17] and [6.18]). But

---

[14] It should be noted that since successive crises did not occur in the same month, this averaging procedure resulted in "leftover" months immediately preceding each crisis, which were omitted from the set of observations used in fitting the regressions, since the leftover months did not comprise full years of data.

the improvement is less marked when $\log_e \bar{t}$ is added to equations involving the rate of business failure liabilities (regressions [6.15] and [6.16]), and its regression coefficient turns out to be non-significant (at the 5 per cent level) in (6.19), in which the lagged business failure rate is introduced. Nor does the introduction of the lagged all-bank suspension rate, as in (6.20), improve the fit noticeably.

Although the results of these regressions fail to confirm clearly the validity of either bank suspensions or time from previous crisis as factors explaining variations in the excess cash reserve ratio of New York banks, the limitations of the data used to measure the two factors are such as to justify withholding final judgment on their net influence. The difficulties in obtaining an adequate measure of bank suspensions have been discussed earlier and are treated at greater length in Appendix C. As far as time elapsed from previous crisis is concerned, the variable $\log_e \bar{t}$ made no allowance for lags in adjustment of desired to actual levels of excess reserves after crisis dates. This is a critical defect, especially when using calendar year data, since there were wide variations in the timing of crises throughout the calendar year, so that, in some instances at least, the discrepancy between desired and actual excess reserves shortly after a crisis may have found reflection in calendar year averages. A lag in adjustment of desired to actual would tend to produce a humplike pattern in the observed excess reserve ratio after crises that cannot be accurately represented by a monotonic function of time since crisis, such as $\log_e t$.

Looking forward to the next chapter, in which monthly data will be employed, time-from-crisis will be introduced in such a way as to allow for lags in adjustment. Further experimentation with bank suspensions and business failure rates is precluded, however, by the unavailability of useful monthly data on these items during the national banking period. But if we can interpret the business failure rate as an approximation to a time series of the risk premium on loans, then this failure rate will find its counterpart in the more direct measures of risk premia introduced in the following chapter.

VII

Empirical Tests: Regressions and Correlations Fitted to Monthly Data for New York Banks 1874–1913, 1921–55

IN THIS CHAPTER are presented the results of a series of tests of the shock and inertia effects on bank asset behavior. First, there will be reported a number of ordinary least squares regression estimates based on the general framework of the model of bank demand for cash developed in Chapter II. These regressions fall into two groups, according to whether it is the shock effect or the inertia effect that is being tested. Second, a series of correlations are presented to examine in greater detail, and from other aspects of bank asset behavior, the operation of the inertia effect. The findings reported in this chapter represent only the most salient results from a rather elaborate program of statistical investigation. To avoid distracting the reader from recognizing the basic outcome of these tests, a large body of technical and statistical detail has been relegated to appendixes. These may be referred to as needed to supplement the text discussion.

THE VARIABLES TO BE TESTED

For convenient reference a brief dictionary of symbols for variables is as follows:[1]

ρ_{e_t} = excess reserves as a percentage of revised deposits

ρ_t = excess reserves plus vault cash as a percentage of revised deposits

r_t = short-term money market interest rate

P_t^a = risk premium based on bond yield spreads, from Macaulay

P_t^m = risk premium based on bond yield spreads, from Moody's

D_{p_t} = current potential deposits

E_t = expected (or "permanent") deposit potential

q_t = transitory deposit potential

A_t = Time elapsed from previous crisis, a shift variable representing the shock effect modified to allow for lagged response to the shift.

[1] More detailed descriptions of these variables will be found in Appendix B. Explanations of data sources and methods for estimating variables are found in Appendix C.

Before turning to the regressions, a brief explanation of the derivation of q_t and A_t is necessary. Transitory potential deposits, q_t, is the difference between current potential deposits and "expected" potential deposits, expressed as a percentage of expected potential deposits. Expected potential deposits is a weighted average of past values of current (or "measured") potential deposits, the weights declining exponentially, according to the formula prescribed by Cagan and Friedman.[2] In this formula the key parameter is β, the coefficient of expectation, which determines the speed at which a given gap between current and expected deposit potential is closed. Its reciprocal, $1/\beta$, is the average length, in months, of the exponential weighting pattern, or the average "memory" period, i.e., the average number of months by which expected deposit potential lags behind actual deposit potential. Of course, β is not known in advance, except perhaps within very wide limits; on the contrary, β is estimated statistically. Inasmuch as different values of β imply different weighted averages of past measured potential deposits, a different time series of q_t is associated with each numerical value of β. Estimating β is equivalent to selecting a "best" q_t time series out of all the alternative series available. By a trial and error process, several regressions are run to select the particular q_t series that produces the highest R^2 for a given regression model. This, in turn, determines the "best" β estimate for that model.

A trial and error estimation procedure is also used in fitting A_t, the shock effect variable.[3] The first step is to select certain liquidity crisis dates.[4] Next, the desired excess reserve ratio caused by the crisis shock is represented by an exponentially decaying transformation of time elapsed from previous crisis of the form $e^{\delta(t_i - t)}$, where t_i is a crisis date, t is a subsequent date, and δ is a parameter that determines how fast the shock effect decays. In Figure 4 the dashed line labeled "desired excess reserve ratio" is a representation of this shock effect except that now the decay is assumed to be exponential rather than linear. By inspection of the pattern of buildup and decline in cash positions of New York banks after crises, δ was assigned a value, common for all crises, of .04167. The final step is to

[2] See Appendix B for a fuller explanation of the rationale for, and the development of, transitory potential deposits.

[3] See Appendix B for a more detailed account of the procedure for estimating A_t, the shock effect variable.

[4] The liquidity crisis dates (t_i) chosen in constructing the A_t variable were September, 1873; May, 1884; August, 1893; October, 1907; October, 1931; January, 1933; and March, 1937. The phrase "liquidity crisis" is used advisedly, since in March, 1937, there was no banking panic per se, although banks engaged in a flurry of selling of investments following the second increase in reserve requirements.

introduce a lag in the adjustment of the actual to the desired excess reserve ratio. This leads to a formula in which the actual excess reserve ratio is a function of A_t, an exponentially weighted average of past values of the desired excess reserve ratio caused by the crisis shock. The weighting pattern depends on the coefficient of adjustment, symbolized by π. This parameter determines the speed at which a given gap between the desired and the actual excess reserve ratio is closed. It is estimated by a trial and error process similar to that used in picking the best value of β. In other words, for selected hypothetical values of π, a set of alternative time series representations of A_t are generated. Each such series is tried in a regression model that makes the actual excess reserve ratio a linear function of A_t. The "best" A_t series is the one that produces the highest R^2, and the "best" value of π is the one that generates this A_t series.

Results of Regression Tests

The statistical fitting of liquidity preference equations for New York City banks proceeds in two ways. First, a series of regressions on observations drawn from "normal" (i.e., non-crisis) periods[5] were run, and the residuals (actual minus predicted) from the most successful of these regressions[6] were used as dependent variables in subsequent regressions testing for the influence of the A_t variable. Second, a series of regressions, using all observations, both for "normal" and crisis periods were run, with ρ_t or ρ_{e_t} as dependent variables.[7] This second series of regressions does *not* include A_t as one of the independent variables.

[5] The normal periods for regressions on New York Clearing House Bank excess cash reserve ratios were: January, 1879–December, 1883; January, 1889–December, 1892; January, 1899–September, 1907; and February, 1911–December, 1913, a total of 248 observations. For regressions on New York City weekly reporting bank excess cash reserve ratios, the periods were: July, 1921–December, 1930, and February, 1948–December, 1951, a total of 161 observations. The period of pegging of Treasury bill rates during and after World War II was eliminated, since this appeared to have led to abnormally low levels of the excess cash reserve ratio.

[6] The residuals in question were calculated for both normal and crisis period observations on the basis of the regressions fitted only to normal period observations.

[7] The running of regressions of ρ_t or ρ_{e_t} on A_t, along with other independent variables for the full set of normal and crisis observations, was not attempted for two reasons. One is that the crisis hypothesis to be tested by A_t says that the effect of a crisis is to cause a shift in the liquidity preference schedules and that, to a first approximation at least, the slope coefficients for variables influencing the demand for excess cash reserves under normal circumstances will not be affected by such a shift.

Another reason is that the identification of the best combination of A_t and q_t series becomes much more complicated when the two sets of series (one set with alternative π weights, the other with alternative β weights) are tested simultaneously in the same regression. By the procedure that was adopted, the best β-weighted q_t series is chosen first on the basis of normal period observations, and only the best π-weighted A_t series remains to be determined from observations on crisis periods.

FIRST REGRESSION SERIES: TESTS OF THE
TIME-ELAPSED-FROM-CRISIS HYPOTHESIS

Table 5 presents the most satisfactory of the regressions run on normal period observations, together with regressions in which the residuals (x_t' or x_t'') derived from the normal period regression equations are dependent variables and A_t is the sole independent variable. Each normal period regression and the corresponding regression on its residuals has the same regression number, the letter A being added to the residuals regression number.

Except for the coefficient of P_t^m all regression coefficients have the right sign and are significant at at least the 1 per cent level by the two-tailed test.[8] This tends to confirm the suggestion made in Chapter II that when the cost of holding money is represented by an interest rate free of default risk such as the Treasury bill yield, the risk premium becomes a superfluous variable. There is little difference between the explanatory power of $1/r_t$ and $\log_e r_t$ judging by the squared correlation coefficients and standard errors statistics in (7.1)–(7.4). Measured by V (the percentage of the total variance in the dependent variable, ρ_t or ρ_{e_t}, for combined normal and crisis periods, that can be explained by [7.1]–[7.4]), it would appear that $1/r_t$ has the edge. This edge is less clear in the A_t regressions. The percentage W, of total variance in ρ_t or ρ_{e_t}, for combined normal and crisis periods, which can be explained by the regressions[9] involving $1/r_t$ (7.1A) and (7.3A) is about equal to the explained variance for paired regressions involving $\log_e r_t$ in the 1874–1913 comparison and somewhat less in the 1921–51 comparison.

The regression parameters for the interest rate variables show little tendency to remain stable between the two periods 1879–1913 and 1921–51. Except for (7.4A), the coefficients for A_t are quite close together. The regression coefficients for the q_t variables display even greater stability, and indicate that a one percentage point change in q_t will be accompanied by a change in ρ_t or ρ_{e_t} for somewhat more than one-tenth of a percentage point—in the same direction.

One particularly interesting result is that the "best" β and π estimates changed considerably between the two periods. The β value rose from .25

[8] Visual inspection as well as Durbin-Watson tests disclose the residuals of our regressions to be serially correlated, so that conditions for the application of the usual tests of significance are not fulfilled. Except in the passage to which this footnote refers, "significance" should be understood to be a shorthand way of indicating that the regression coefficient is more than three times its standard error.

[9] Note that $W = (1 - V\rho)R_x^2 + V\rho$, where the subscripts ρ and x serve to identify the regressions in each pair of normal period and residual regressions to which the statistic refers. Thus, for regression (7.1) and (7.1A), $W = (1 - .543).468 + .545 = .757$.

TABLE 5
REGRESSIONS, NEW YORK BANKS, 1874-1951
(Monthly Data)

REGRESSION NUMBER	TIME PERIOD COVERED	NUMBER OF OBSERVATIONS	DEPENDENT VARIABLE	CONSTANT TERM	COEFFICIENTS, STANDARD ERRORS (IN PARENTHESES) OF INDEPENDENT VARIABLES, β VALUES OF q_t VARIABLES (IN BRACKETS) AND π VALUES OF A_t VARIABLES (IN BRACKETS)						GOODNESS OF FIT AND PREDICTION		
					A_t	$1/r_t$	$\log_e r_t$	P_t^a	P_t^m	q_t	R^2	V	W
7.1.....	Normal Periods, 1879–1913	248	ρ_t	0.342	....	2.29 (.66)	....	2.06 (.24)	....	.144 (.017) [.25]	.545	.543	......
7.2.....	Normal Periods, 1879–1913	248	ρ_t	1.921	....	....	−.70 (.18)	2.09 (.24)	....	.141 (.016) [.25]	.551	.511	......
7.3.....	Normal Periods, 1921–51	161	ρ	0.237	....	.493 (.063)	....	....	.012 (.031)	.127 (.013) [.90]	.521	.569	......
7.4.....	Normal Periods, 1921–51	161	ρe_t	0.678	....	....	−.191 (.026)	....	−.011 (.030)	.123 (.014) [.90]	.501	.448	......
7.1A....	Aug.'74–Dec.'13	472	x_t'	−0.146	10.533 (.517) [.20]	....	....	....	....	....	.468	......	.757
7.2A....	Aug.'74–Dec.'13	472	x_t'	−0.173	10.774 (.525) [.20]	....	....	....	....	....	.471	......	.741
7.3A....	July'21–Dec.'51	366	x_t'	−0.813	11.988 (1.118) [.025]	....	....	....	....	....	.240	......	.672
7.4A....	July'21–Dec.'51	366	x_t'	−2.400	29.550 (1.382) [.02]	....	....	....	....	....	.556	......	.755

to .90, which implies that the average length of lag in expectations shortened from 4 months to 1.1 months. This is consistent with the general presumption that gradual development of money market institutions and instruments has increased the speed with which banks react to changes in their reserve positions. Included in this development are the changes wrought through the Federal Reserve System—for example, the greater flexibility in adjustment to disturbances that has been made possible by the Federal Reserve's discounting facility, by the development of the federal funds market,[10] and the lessened short-run instability in bank reserves that has, with the exception of some episodes, accompanied Federal Reserve administration of the stock of high-powered money.

On the other hand, the regressions show a decline in the π value from .20 to .02 or .025, which implies a lengthening of the lag in adjustment of desired to actual cash positions under crisis conditions. In other words, whereas the average lag in adjustment of actual to desired excess reserve ratios was five months after crises during the 1874–1913 period, it was forty to fifty months in the crises of the 1930's. This is a surprising result; there would seem to be no strong reasons for supposing that institutional changes caused a retardation of the rate at which banks could adjust actual to desired cash positions.

Examination of the residuals generated from these regressions reveal another shortcoming of the crisis-shock model. In both the (7.1A) and (7.2A) regressions, the residuals (actual minus predicted) tend to show large positive values in all immediate postcrisis periods with the exception of the post–1907 crisis, when the residuals turn sharply negative. (See Figure 9 panels C and D.) It cannot be argued that this strong reversal of the behavior of residuals after 1907 is simply the result of failure of the model to take account of the milder nature of the 1907 crisis, so that the predicted values of excess reserves after 1907 represent estimates based on an average of crisis experience that is heavily weighted by the more drastic dislocations of 1873, 1884, and 1893. Unfortunately, the notion that 1907 was a mild crisis is erroneous; judging by the volume of bank failures, the extent to which banks resorted to restriction of cash payments, and the general public attitude as to its relative severity, the 1907 crisis must rank among the most serious of the financial upheavals during

---

[10] It may be thought that these developments would have their main impact on the "adjustment" coefficient as distinct from the "expectations" coefficient. But insofar as these institutional developments make banks better able to control the level of their reserves by their own actions, then by that token, they are better able to offset some of the true transitory variation in their reserves. As mentioned before, it may be preferable to take some other reserves measure, such as unborrowed reserves, to get at "true" transitory reserves.

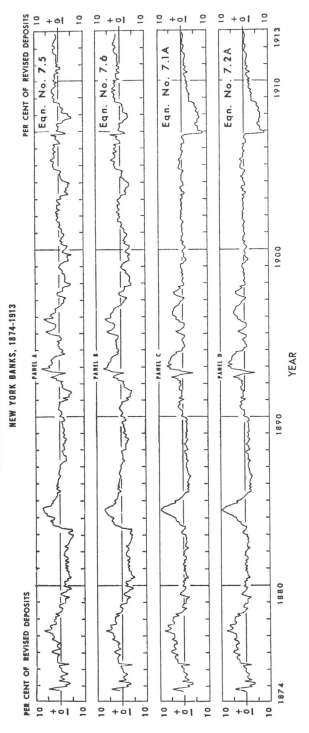

RESIDUALS FROM SELECTED REGRESSIONS

NEW YORK BANKS, 1874-1913

PER CENT OF REVISED DEPOSITS

Eqn. No. 7.5

Eqn. No. 7.6

Eqn. No. 7.1A

Eqn. No. 7.2A

PANEL A

PANEL B

PANEL C

PANEL D

PER CENT OF REVISED DEPOSITS

YEAR

FIG. 9

the period of national banking. By comparison with the gale of 1907, the crisis of 1884 was no more than a zephyr.

Again, the residuals of (7.3A) and (7.4A) (panels C and D, Figure 10) indicate that the predicted shock effect falls wide of the mark, particularly in 1939–41. Moreover, the large negative residuals in 1933 and 1937 cannot be explained as reflecting short-term lags in response to sharp declines in potential deposits inasmuch as the fitting of (7.3) and (7.4) for normal periods allows for this lag by including q_t (transitory potential deposits) as a variable.

Possibly the disappointing results of these tests of the shock hypothesis are the result of various specification errors—improper dating of crises, failure to include a parameter to measure "degree of trauma," incorrect choice of the mathematical form of the decay function, oversimplificaiton in the model of adjustment of actual to desired quantities, and so forth. After all, despite its crudities, about half of the variance in excess reserve ratios after crises can be explained by the shock effect regression model. But if this version of the shift hypothesis is adjudged a failure, then the view that after crises banks moved along stable liquidity preference functions must also be rejected, since the unexplained residuals include variations in bank excess cash ratios that interest rate effects could not explain.

169 45c

SECOND REGRESSION SERIES: TESTS OF THE INERTIA EFFECT MODEL

If the shock effect model is not an overwhelming success in predicting postcrisis excess reserve ratios, does the inertia effect do any better? Evidence now to be presented suggests that the answer is yes, but with some qualifications. While the inertia model can explain variations in bank cash during postcrisis periods better than the shock model, it does so at the expense of making poor predictions during normal periods. The reason for this, as will become apparent, is that the onset of a liquidity crisis tends to affect drastically one of the key parameters in the inertia model, namely, the coefficient of expectation, β. After allowing for crisis-induced changes in β (and a secular drift in β during normal periods), the inertia model supports the view that forces which influence bank demand for cash during postcrisis periods can also explain variations in bank cash positions under normal circumstances. The findings suggest that the theory of bank demand for cash presented in Chapter II is adequate to explain bank behavior under a wide variety of conditions.

The most satisfactory regressions of those used to test the inertia effect are presented in Table 6.[11] In these regressions all months, both for normal

[11] Appendix D contains several tables and related commentary reporting numerous other regressions testing the inertia effect in conjunction with other independent variables from the list on page 92, and for various subperiods.

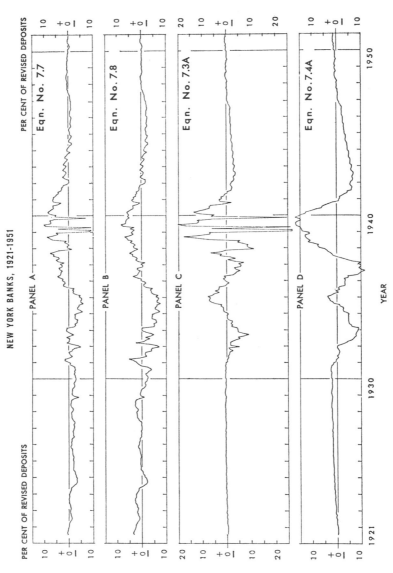

RESIDUALS FROM SELECTED REGRESSIONS

NEW YORK BANKS, 1921-1951

PANEL A — Eqn. No. 7.7

PANEL B — Eqn. No. 7.8

PANEL C — Eqn. No. 7.3A

PANEL D — Eqn. No. 7.4A

PER CENT OF REVISED DEPOSITS

YEAR

FIG. 10

periods and postcrisis periods, were included. Separate regressions were run for the periods September, 1874–November, 1913 and July, 1921–December, 1951.

These regressions, like those reported in Table 5, disclose statistically significant interest rate effects on bank cash positions. Part of the reason for larger cash ratios in postcrisis periods was that the cost of holding excess cash declined during these interludes. This is not to say, however,

TABLE 6

REGRESSIONS, NEW YORK BANKS, 1874–1951[a]

(Monthly Data)

EQUATION NUMBER	TIME PERIOD COVERED	NUMBER OF OBSERVATIONS	DEPENDENT VARIABLE	CONSTANT TERM	COEFFICIENTS, STANDARD ERRORS (IN PARENTHESES) OF INDEPENDENT VARIABLES, AND β VALUES OF q_t VARIABLES (IN BRACKETS)[b]					R^2
					$1/r_t$	$\log_e r_t$	P_t^a	P_t^m	q_t	
7.5...	Sept. '74–Nov. '13	470	ρ_t	−4.598	9.118 (.910)	....	7.71 (.35)	......	.119 (.012) [.025]	.713
7.6...	Sept. '74–Nov. '13	470	ρ_t	0.264	......	−1.65 (.26)	8.07 (.36)	......	.169 (.010) [.025]	.679
7.7...	July '21–Dec. '51	366	ρ_{e_t}	2.414	.212 (.014)	....	......	.523 (.166)	.212 (.008) [.02]	.859
7.8...	July '21–Dec. '51	366	ρ_{e_t}	3.569	......	−2.074 (.012)	......	.197 (.160)	.195 (.008) [.02]	.874

[a] Note that ρ_{e_t}, q_t are not seasonally adjusted, December, 1942–December, 1947. During World War II, beginning in December, 1942, and extending through August, 1947, periodic War Loan and Victory Loan bond drives, changes in the required reserve status of Treasury war loan deposits at commercial banks, and changes in pegging policy, operate in such a manner as to thwart straightforward seasonal adjustment procedures, as applied to ρ_{e_t} or $D\rho_t$. Instead of making ad hoc attempts to meticulously remove or smooth the jumps or semiregular fluctuations of these series it was decided to let them stand in unadjusted form.

[b] The q_t series shown for (7.7) and (7.8) is not necessarily optimal. No q_t series with β weight of less than .02 was tried; the "best" fits, among the alternative q_t series tested, were obtained with $\beta = .02$.

that a liquidity trap existed at such times. The findings do not give much support to the liquidity trap hypothesis—which was interpreted earlier as at the very least requiring the interest elasticity of bank demand for cash to be greater at low interest rates than at high interest rates.

The evidence comes from comparisons of computed elasticities. For the pre-Federal Reserve period, the elasticity of ρ_t with respect to r_t, when evaluated at the means of the ρ_t and $1/r_t$ observations used in fitting (7.1) is −.266, whereas the same elasticity, evaluated at the means of the

ρ_t and $1/r_t$ observations used in fitting (7.5) is $-.644$.[12] Since the means of ρ_t and $1/r_t$ are greater in (7.5) than in (7.1), this result would suggest that the interest elasticity of the excess cash reserve ratio increases as the interest rate level falls. But the comparison of (7.2) and (7.6) shows the opposite result. The elasticity, when measured at the mean of ρ_t, is $-.292$ in (7.2) while it is only $-.181$ in (7.6).[13] The average interest rate is, of course, lower in (7.6).

The comparisons for the Federal Reserve period 1921–51 are similarly inconclusive. In (7.8) the interest elasticity is $-.463$, while in the corresponding regression (7.4), which excludes depression and wartime observations, the elasticity is slightly lower ($-.450$), thus tending to support the liquidity trap hypothesis. The interest elasticity estimated from (7.7), however, is $-.025$, measured at the means of ρ_t and $1/r_t$, whereas if only normal period observations are used, as in (7.3), the estimated elasticity is $-.475$, contrary to the liquidity trap prediction.

The results, then, are an almost perfect standoff as to whether or not interest elasticity of demand for bank cash increases as interest rates decline. When it is remembered that an inverse relation between interest elasticity and the level of interest rates is merely a necessary but not sufficient condition for the existence of a liquidity trap, these findings cast serious doubt on this hypothesis, as applied to U.S. banking experience.

Once again, as in previously discussed normal period regressions (7.1)–(7.4), the default risk variable, P_t^m, shows considerably less explanatory power for the 1921–51 period than does its counterpart, P_t^a, for the pre-Federal Reserve era. It will be recalled that this could be attributed to the use of the risk-free yield on short-term governments to represent r_t for most of the 1921–51 period. During the 1920's, however, the call loan rate is used, and insofar as a risk premium may be embodied in this interest rate, it may have contributed to the statistical significance of P_t^m in (7.7).

The bond grade yield spread, P_t^a, operates very much like a trend factor during the national banking era. Throughout this era, the spread between

[12] The elasticity is

$$\frac{r}{\rho}\frac{\partial \rho}{\partial r} = \frac{r}{\rho}\left(-\frac{b}{r^2}\right) = -\frac{b}{r\rho},$$

where b is the regression coefficient.

[13] The elasticity is

$$\frac{r}{\rho}\cdot\frac{\partial \rho}{\partial r} = \frac{r}{\rho}\left(\frac{\partial \rho}{\partial \ln r}\cdot\frac{\partial \ln r}{\partial r}\right) = \frac{a}{\rho},$$

where a is the regression coefficient (i.e., $\partial \rho/\partial \ln r$). At low interest rates, ρ is presumably greater than at high interest rates, so this elasticity is inversely related to r.

low- and high-grade railroad bond yields narrowed, with only minor set-
backs in major depressions. The narrowing of the spread was especially
rapid just after the turn of the twentieth century.[14] One of the principal
effects of the inclusion of the bond grade yield spread in regressions for the
pre-Federal Reserve era was to alter the sign of the regression coefficients
for the short-term interest rate; when the bond grade yield spread is
dropped, the coefficients for the short-term interest rate tend to have
positive signs, contrary to theory. Yet, for subintervals of time during
this era, correlations between the short-term interest rate and the excess
cash reserve ratio are regularly negative (see Table 8). There appeared to
be a secular downward shift in the ratio of excess cash to deposits. The
bond grade yield spread, aside from its statistical effectiveness in accounting for this shift, possesses a clearly justifiable theoretical validity, as has
been demonstrated in Chapter II. Objections may be lodged against the
particular measures that have been chosen to reflect default risk, but the
general direction of cyclical and secular movements of the P_t series are in
accord with patterns that a priori judgment and casual observation suggest to be appropriate for a default risk variable.

A finding of the greatest importance for this study is that the β value
of the "best" q_t series is drastically different when the task is to explain
only non-crisis variations in the cash ratio than it is when the task is to explain both postcrisis and normal variations. The estimated β values of .025
or .02 indicated by (7.5)–(7.8) are not representative of the response pattern of banks during normal periods. Equations (7.1)–(7.4), which were
fitted only to non-crisis months, indicate β values of .25 or .90. Thus in
normal periods the average expectations lag is estimated at one to four
months, but for all periods, normal and postcrisis combined, the expectations lag lengthens to forty or fifty months. Clearly the latter estimates
are not at all representative of the response pattern of banks during
normal periods. The trial and error fitting process for (7.5)–(7.8) tends to
select a weighting pattern for q_t that applies to postcrisis fluctuations in
ρ_t, because these contribute a high proportion of the total variance in ρ_t
over crisis and normal periods combined. This shows up very clearly in
the regression residuals graphed in Figures 9 and 10. In normal periods,
the residuals for (7.1A)–(7.4A) are noticeably smaller than the residuals
for (7.5)–(7.8). For normal periods the residuals for (7.1A)–(7.4A) are

---

[14] P. Cagan, *Determinants and Effects of Changes in the Money Stock, 1875–1955*
(New York: National Bureau of Economic Research, 1965), pp. 213–19, attributes the
decline in the excess reserve ratio of banks after 1900 to the development of Treasury
policies aimed at monetary stabilization. Cagan's hypothesis is that Treasury actions
after 1900 operated to reduce economic uncertainty, particularly with respect to bank
reserves, and that this led banks to desire less cash in relation to deposits. On our analysis, the decline can be ascribed to reduced default risks or risk aversion.

virtually identical with those for (7.1)–(7.4), since the shock effect variable A_t has almost no influence during normal periods.

During postcrisis periods, it appears that New York banks characteristically lengthened the time span they considered in estimating their expected or "permanent" deposit potential. Thus, if they experienced a sharp inflow of reserve funds shortly after the crisis has passed, they tended to regard much of the increment to their deposit potential as transitory. In consequence, New York banks tended to be extremely cautious in putting the increment to work. But although they increased the amounts of their excess reserves, these banks also sought outlets in lending—particularly in short-term highly liquid money market claims such as call loans, acceptances, commercial paper, and so forth. This helped to force down short-term interest rates.

Concluding Observations on Regression Tests

Comparison of the relative predicting ability of the shock effect and inertia effect models tends to favor the inertia explanation. Although the inertia effect equations (7.5)–(7.6) explain less of the total variance in excess cash ratios than the shock effect (7.1A)–(7.2A) in the pre-Federal Reserve era, the difference is not large and is mainly due to the superior predictions made during normal periods, not crisis periods. This merely suggests that the inertia hypothesis should be modified to allow for variations in β, the expectations coefficient, between normal and crisis periods. As for the crisis periods themselves, Figure 9 shows that the shock effect equations fail entirely to explain the very modest accumulation of excess reserves by New York banks following the 1907 panic. In other postcrisis periods the superiority of the inertia effect equations in producing smaller residuals is still evident but is much less pronounced. Turning to the 1921–51 period, the inertia effect (7.7)–(7.8) performs better than the shock effect (7.3A)–(7.4A) both in terms of percentage of total variance of excess reserve ratios explained and in terms of producing smaller residuals during the crisis period of the 1930's.

The inertia hypothesis is not an overwhelmingly superior model, however. The fit of the inertia equation is not outstandingly good and there is an obviously strong serial correlation in the residuals of these equations. Clearly there is considerable room for refinement of the model. Especially suggestive of the sort of improvement that seems most needed is the apparent instability of the β coefficient. The value of β, which leads to the best fitting regression, is very different in normal periods than it is in postcrisis periods. In a more elaborate model, it should be possible to integrate the shock effect and the inertia effect in a framework that permits the lag in expectations to vary as a function of observable variables.[15]

RESULTS OF CORRELATION TESTS

To examine this apparent instability in the β parameter more closely, it was decided to subdivide the long time spans used for the regression analyses into periods of a few years in length and to correlate ρ_{e_t} with various alternative β weighted q_t series. Table 7, which presents the results of this correlation analysis, does, indeed, disclose a pattern of variation in the β value that produces the maximum correlation between q_t and ρ_{e_t}. After each crisis, the β value of the "best" q_t series[16] declines. This happens after the crises of 1873, 1884, 1893, and 1907. It can also be observed that in each successive postcrisis period through 1907, the value of β for the correlation-maximizing q_t series is greater than in the previous postcrisis period. After 1907, the decline in β for the "best" series is negligible.

It is tempting to speculate on the causes of this gradual change in behavior of the New York Clearing House Banks. One possibility is that these banks became more and more accustomed to crises and to the measures required to bring them to an end. It is also possible that the banks came to believe that once a crisis had passed, the probability of an early recurrence of panic conditions was not much higher than if the crisis had not occurred at all.

Again, in the 1930's, the advent of bank panic conditions is accompanied by a decline in the β value for the "best" q_t series. This implies that banks, in forming their expectations as to the "permanent" level of potential deposits, tend to lengthen the period of past experience that they deem relevant, whenever bank panic strikes. And it is because of this lengthening of the "memory period" that movements of the excess reserve ratio and current potential deposits Dp_t tend to be so highly cor-

[15] Thus the demand function might be written

$$\rho_t = f(r_t, q_t, P_t, A_t) \,,$$

and the expectations adjustment equation, adapted from an approach used by Maurice Allais in an unpublished study of the demand for money, might be written

$$\frac{dE_t}{dt} = \frac{\beta}{\rho_t}(Dp_t - E_t), \qquad \text{where} \qquad q_t = \frac{Dp_t - E_t}{E_t}.$$

Since the expectations lag as we have observed it tends to be greatest when ρ_t is large, this model has the desirable property of taking this into account.

[16] The "best" q_t series as determined by simple correlation need not be the same as the "best" q_t series as determined by R^2 in a multiple regression.

related in postcrisis periods, whereas in other periods the correlation is sometimes small or even negative (see Table 7).

At this point it is pertinent to take up the issue of spurious correlation, particularly spurious correlation of ratios. As indicated in Appendix E correlation of p_t with q_t may lead to an overestimate of the true (positive) correlation coefficient because both variables contain a common element, R_t (total reserves), that is subject to measurement error. Also, the tendency will be to underestimate the true value of β, insofar as the correlation of common elements in the numerators of the p_t and q_t ratios dominates the correlation of common elements in the denominators.

It is possible to get an impression of the extent of this bias by comparison of Tables 7 and 8. In Table 8, the denominator of the q_t ratio (i.e., E_t, or expected deposit potential) has been correlated with total deposits subject to reserve, which is roughly equivalent to the denominator of the p_t ratio. While spurious positive correlation still exists, the direction of the bias in estimates of the "best" β is reversed. Changes in total reserves tend to be accompanied by corresponding changes in total deposits subject to reserve (except when the changes in reserves are associated with changes in borrowings or capital), and if there are errors of measurement in R_t, they will tend to be reflected in total deposits subject to reserve also.[17] The influence of these errors will be in the direction of overestimating β, that is, in the direction of picking a "best" E_t series in which the *current* value of deposit potential, Dp_t, is given too large a weight. Consequently, we can expect the time horizon of banks to be underestimated by the correlations of Table 8.

Period-by-period comparison of Tables 7 and 8 tends to confirm this reasoning. In only one matching period, September, 1876–March, 1884, does the "best" β weight in Table 8 fail to equal or exceed the corresponding "best" β weight in Table 7. But the broad patterns of fluctuation in this best β weight are seen to be similar between the two tables. In particular, the progressively smaller decline in the best postcrisis β weight during the period of national banking shows up again in Table 8. And the same tendency for the β value in the 1930's to fall is shown in Table 8, except that the decline does not register until after December, 1933.

As a final step in our empirical analysis, it is instructive to reexamine the Horwich-Kilberg analysis of changes in earning assets and changes in effective reserves, with the use of the concept of expected potential deposits. In Table 9, the various selected E_t series are correlated with total

---

[17] By reason of the balance sheet identity. It is possible that part of the errors could show up in borrowings or capital or in loans and investments, of course.

TABLE 7

Coefficients of Simple Correlation of the New York Banks' Excess Cash Reserve Ratio with Short-Term Interest Rate, Current Deposit Potential of New York Banks and Transitory Deposit Potential of New York Banks

Period	Dp_t	q_t for Selected Values of β											$\log_e r_t$
		.01	.02	.025	.033	.05	.10	.15	.25	.50	1.0	2.0	
Aug. '74–Aug. '76	.617	.653[a]	.650	.649	.643	.631	.576	.525	.460	.381	.307	.249	−.314
Sept. '76–Mar. '84	−.335	...	...	−.247	−.259	−.228	.072	.025	.114	.179	.201[a]	.195	−.339
Apr. '84–Mar. '87	.886	.964	.981	.984[a]	.983	.974	.932	.887	.797	.640	.506	.423	−.868
Apr. '87–July '93	.559	.621	.626	.627	.626	.629	.666	.695	.710[a]	.686	.619	.553	−.639
Aug. '93–July '96	.889	...	...	.974	.980	.986[a]	.973	.938	.847	.670	.494	.670	−.769
Aug. '96–Feb. '02	−.580	...	...	.070	.134	.245	.506	.625	.666[a]	.593	.486	.407	−.595
Mar. '02–Sept. '07	.382	...	...	.675	.689	.719	.782	.813	.829[a]	.797	.717	.627	−.342
Oct. '07–Sept. '10	.714	...	...	.738	.745	.754	.768	.776[a]	.770	.702	.598	.510	−.629
Oct. '10–Dec. '13	.390	...	...	.669	.681	.710	.789	.846	.871[a]	.802	.670	.567	−.589
Mar. '19–Dec. '21	.570	...	...	.691	.693	.696[a]	.695	.684	.648	.578	.486	.420	−.046
Jan. '22–Sept. '31	−.666	...	...	−.283	−.221	−.080	.188	.297	.372	.400[a]	.393	.385	−.072
Oct. '31–Dec. '33[b]	.928	.983[a]	.945	.934	.939	.946	.954[a]	.945	.901	.776	.635	.533	−.728
Jan. '34–June '37[b]	.941	.978	.991[a]	.918	.871	.782	.608	.517	.424	.338	.278	.232	−.608
July '37–Dec. '42[b]	.785	...	...	.991	.985	.967	.876	.774	.609	.251	.397	.192	−.845
Jan. '43–Dec. '46[b]	.153	...	...	.043	−.065	−.157	−.144	.015	.152[a]	.147	.049	−.026	−.403
Jan. '47–Dec. '51[b]	.432	...	...	.225	.238	.181	.174	.236	.296	.321	.333[a]	.319	.457
Feb. '48–Mar. '51	.195	.318	.288	.272	.255	.252	.262	.297	.369	.431	.454[a]	...	−.235
Jan. '52–Dec. '55	.417	...	...	.755	.775	.801	.845	.867	.877[a]	.835	.708	.603	−.235
Apr. '51–Nov. '55	.190	.734	.663	.672	.707	.753	.804	.818[a]	.814	.766	.668	...	−.243

[a] Indicates maximum positive correlation among the q_t variables that were tested.   [b] ρ_t, q_t, and Dp_t not seasonally adjusted, January, 1932, through December, 1947.

107

TABLE 8

COEFFICIENTS OF SIMPLE CORRELATION OF TOTAL DEPOSITS SUBJECT TO RESERVE WITH CURRENT AND EXPECTED DEPOSIT POTENTIAL, NEW YORK BANKS

PERIOD	Dp_t	E_t FOR SELECTED VALUES OF β											
		.01	.02	.025	.033	.05	.10	.15	.25	.50	1.0	1.4	2.0
Aug. '74–Aug. '76	.420	−.769	−.716	−.649	−.208	.754a	.733	.676	.589	.489	.450	.441	.432
Sept. '76–Mar. '84	.866	.899	.821	.772	.729	.743	.838	.879	.905	.909a	.896	.887	.878
Apr. '84–Mar. '87	.494	.730	.780	.797	.827	.872	.927a	.900	.803	.665	.573	.542	.518
Apr. '87–July '93	.944	.738	.738	.732	.717	.709	.804	.875	.939	.973a	.968	.961	.954
Aug. '93–July '96	.794	.228	.321	.362	.429	.548	.789	.887	.931a	.909	.860	.836	.817
Aug. '96–Feb. '02	.955	.936	.940	.942	.946	.956	.977	.985	.987a	.980	.970	.965	.961
Mar. '02–Sept. '07	.953	.541	.581	.601	.633	.696	.828	.899	.957	.982a	.975	.968	.961
Oct. '07–Sept. '10	.879	.113	.184	.218	.269	.368	.606	.761	.902	.954a	.929	.912	.896
Oct. '10–Nov. '13	.837	.194	.259	.299	.360	.487	.741	.853	.932	.935a	.893	.875	.858
Mar. '19–Dec. '21	.945	−.597	−.460	−.363	−.120	.400	.840	.896	.934	.955	.956a	.954	.950
Jan. '22–Sept. '31b	.986	.942	.937	.937	.939	.948	.966	.974	.983	.991	.992a	.991	.989
Oct. '31–Dec. '33b	.762	.207	.318	.378	.461	.540	.633	.687	.748	.798	.805a	.799	.785
Jan. '34–June '37b	.535	.971	.980	.983	.988	.993a	.975	.932	.839	.702	.607	.578	.556
July '37–Dec. '42b	.627	.968	.975	.977	.978a	.972	.919	.859	.777	.695	.652	.642	.634
Jan. '43–Jan '48b	.981	.843	.699	.019	.391	−.299	.473	.773	.890	.939	.966	.974	.979a
Feb. '48–Dec. '51	.945	.658	.693	.729	.771	.805	.831	.839	.882	.925	.955	.956a	.953
Jan. '52–Nov. '55	.883	.666	.688	.700	.710	.737	.815	.878	.939	.959a	.931	.915	.901
Jul. '21–Nov. '55	.839	.992a	.989	.981	.967	.941	.899	.879	.862	.849	.843	.841	.840

a Indicates maximum positive correlation among E_t variables that were tested.

b Dp_t, E_t, and Total Deposits Subject to Reserve not seasonally adjusted, January, 1932 through December, 1947.

108

TABLE 9

Coefficients of Simple Correlation of Total Loans and Investments with Current and Expected Deposit Potential, New York Banks

Period	Dp_t	E_t for Selected Values of β											
		.01	.02	.025	.033	.05	.10	.15	.25	.50	1.0	1.4	2.0
Mar. '19–Dec. '21	.910	−.712	−.552	−.437	−.166	.424	.912	.962	.975[a]	.962	.940	.929	.921
Jan. '22–Sept. '31	.954	.978[a]	.976	.976	.975	.975	.972	.970	.968	.967	.963	.961	.958
Oct. '31–Dec. '33[b]	.375	.094	.085	.178	.327	.479	.586[a]	.580	.554	.508	.456	.433	.408
Jan. '34–June '37[b]	.392	.950	.958	.961	.964[a]	.963	.930	.873	.759	.592	.476	.442	.416
July '37–Dec. '42[b]	.192	.945[a]	.924	.912	.888	.832	.663	.537	.397	.278	.222	.209	.200
Jan. '43–Jan. '48[b]	.068	.165	−.280	−.755	−.741	−.733	−.466	−.163	.026	.080	.080[a]	.077	.072
Feb. '48–Dec. '51	.830	.769	.771	.774	.774	.751	.667	.671	.743	.813	.847[a]	.847	.841
Jan. '52–Nov. '55	.747	.893	.903	.909	.914	.924	.945	.950[a]	.934	.885	.811	.787	.769

[a] Indicates maximum positive correlation among E_t variables that were tested.

[b] Dp_t, E_t, and loans and investments not seasonally adjusted, January, 1932, through December, 1947.

loans and investments of New York weekly reporting banks.[18] In these correlations the errors in measurement, if anything, are likely to produce negative spurious correlation between E_t and loans and investments. The results run sharply counter to the notion that during the middle and late 1930's, increments to reserves, when translated by the banks into increments to expected potential deposits, were not put to work through expansion of loans and investments. In fact, the puzzling periods in this table are not the 1930's, but rather the 1920's and the 1943–48 period. During the 1920's, it would appear that almost any weight from .01 to 2.0 would do about equally well. The selection of the extremely long memory period of one hundred months (1/.01) is therefore to be taken with a grain of salt. The 1943–48 period presents a somewhat different problem; here the puzzle is why the correlation coefficient for the best E_t series is so low. It would seem that during much of this period, New York banks did not regard their reserves or total deposit potential as an important constraining influence on their portfolio decisions. Since the result of pegging government security prices was to allow banks themselves to determine the volume of reserves they wished to hold, the more relevant constraints during this period were interest rates facing banks, changes in the volume of government securities outstanding, and short-run changes in required reserves emanating from the periodic war loan drives.

CONCLUSION

The regressions reported in this chapter attempt to distinguish between variations in excess reserves of a group of American banks that can be attributed to movements along a demand schedule relating excess reserves to the short-term interest rate and variations that can be assigned to shifts of that demand schedule.

In regard to movements along the demand schedule, attention centers not so much on the numerical values of the interest elasticities as on the estimated elasticities at different levels of interest rates or excess reserve ratios. A necessary but not sufficient condition for the existence of a liquidity trap with respect to the desired excess reserve ratio is that the estimated elasticity be higher at low interest rates (and high excess reserve ratios) than at high interest rates (and low excess reserve ratios). In view of these rather liberal requirements, the results are unfavorable to the liquidity trap. Depending on whether one fits regressions in which the interest rate has been subjected to a logarithmic transformation or to a reciprocal transformation, it can be inferred that the interest elasticity

[18] Data on total loans and investments are not available for New York Clearing House Banks.

of demand is either higher or lower at low interest rates in both the national banking era and the 1921–51 period. If elasticities had consistently turned out to be lower in normal periods than in combined normal and crisis periods, there would have been confirming evidence for the liquidity trap, inasmuch as interest rates were higher on average during normal periods. But the results showed in about half of the comparisons that this was not the case. Moreover, the estimated elasticities are, in all cases, less than unity when measured at the means, so that the evidence of increasing elasticity is hardly the same as evidence of a liquidity trap in the usual sense of an elasticity approaching infinity.

A number of variables were tested for their influence as factors tending to shift the desired excess reserve ratio of banks viewed as a function of the short-term interest rate. Taken as a group they reflect various hypotheses proposed as alternatives to the liquidity trap explanation of variations in the excess reserve ratio. Included in this group were:[19] (a) spreads between yields on low- and high-grade bonds interpreted as measures of risk premiums or expected defaults on low-grade earning assets; (b) spreads between long-term and short-term interest rates interpreted as liquidity premiums or expected gains or losses from holding long-term investments; (c) penalty rates on forced sale of earning assets or emergency borrowing, as represented by the Federal Reserve discount rate or federal funds rate; (d) exponential transformation of time elapsed from dates of previous banking crisis to reflect banking crisis shock effects; (e) expected drains and inflows, as measured by transitory potential deposits or the current rate of change in potential deposits; (f) lags in adjustment of desired to actual levels of the excess reserve ratio as reflected in regression models involving the lagged dependent variable or rates of change in the dependent variables; and (g) miscellaneous shift factors, including a dummy variable to reflect alteration of the liquidity characteristics of government securities during a period of "pegged" prices, and a time trend variable to represent the secular influence of various economies in the management of bank cash positions. Among these variables, the most successful performers were the spread between low- and high-grade bond yields and transitory deposit potential. The bond yield spread acts primarily as a trend factor explaining the downtrend in the excess reserve ratio during the national banking era. The shock effect variable works fairly satisfactorily in explaining excess cash ratios in the postcrisis periods following 1884 and 1893, but fails adequately to predict the pattern of variation in cash ratios after the 1907 crisis and in the years following the

---

[19] See Appendix D for regression tests on variables not reported on in this chapter.

bank holiday of 1933. As shown in Appendix D, lags in adjustment of desired to actual excess reserve ratios do not, in themselves, add much to the explanation of excess reserve ratios.[20]

By all odds, the most effective explanatory variable uncovered in this study was transitory deposit potential. With the exception of a few periods, expected inflows or outflows of cash, as measured by transitory deposit potential, proved to be an important if not the most important factor contribution to variations in the excess reserve ratio. The main role of the transitory deposit potential variable in the present study resides in its contribution to the explanation of movements in excess cash ratios subsequent to bank panics. After each major banking crisis since 1873, New York banks experienced sharp increases in their total deposit potential. In some instances deposit potential doubled or even tripled in the year following the crisis date. But even such extreme fluctuations as these could account for only a small fraction of the observed variations in excess reserve ratios without the expectational lag reflected in transitory deposit potential. The transitory deposit potential variable is capable of explaining the relatively modest rise in excess cash reserve ratios after the 1907 crisis, the much more lengthy period of high excess reserve ratios in the 1930's than in other postcrisis periods, the timing of peaks in postcrisis cash ratios, and the moderate rise in interest rates coupled with the sluggish response of bank loans to the doubling of reserve requirements in 1936–37, all of which pose thorny problems for other proposed explanations of postcrisis behavior of New York banks.

[20] Unless one chooses to interpret transitory potential deposits as evidence of a lag in adjustment of desired to actual cash. It is worth noting that Meigs, in his investigation of the demand for free reserves, failed to find a strong partial correlation between the free reserve ratio and the rate of change in that ratio, although his approximation to the instantaneous rate of change was closer than ours (see regressions [T.14]–[T.16], as reported in A. J. Meigs, *Free Reserves and the Money Supply* [Chicago: University of Chicago Press, 1962], Appendix A). Consequently, one would be justified in concluding that the lag in adjusting the actual excess reserve ratio to the desired ratio is negligible, under ordinary conditions.

VIII

Summary

THE DEMAND by commercial banks for cash in excess of reserve requirements plays an important role in theories of monetary policy. Whether one adopts a quantity theory framework, the Federal Reserve's "reserve position" doctrine, or a Keynesian theory of interest rate determination, one's explanation of the workings of the monetary system would not be complete without an analysis of the factors determining the fraction of total cash reserves held in excess of reserve requirements (or an equivalent analysis). In any of these theoretical contexts the effectiveness of Federal Reserve monetary policy depends to a significant degree on the existence of predictably stable equilibrium excess reserve positions, so that commercial banks act as reliable intermediaries in the transmission of monetary changes to the rest of the economy. Yet, a review of discussions of banks' excess reserve behavior shows that in the past four decades prevailing opinion swung, in pendulum fashion, from the view that banks sought an equilibrium level of zero excess reserves to the view that there was no stable equilibrium level, and then swung back again to essentially the original opinion. This cycle parallels the behavior of member bank excess reserves themselves, which climbed to unprecedented levels in the years 1934–40, then rapidly fell back to the negligible amounts that had characterized the 1920's.

THE LIQUIDITY TRAP

The dominant diagnosis of banks during the 1930's has been that no amount of central bank action to increase bank reserves would have induced banks to expand their loans and investments faster, because for all intents and purposes, the banks were in a liquidity trap. It has been alleged that interest rates and the borrower demand for bank credit were both at such low ebb that banks really had no choice but to accumulate excess reserves as total bank reserves increased. In terms of the familiar liquidity preference schedule, the curve depicting desired excess reserves (expressed as a ratio to deposits, and as a function of, say, the short-term rate of interest) would be infinitely interest elastic at some low, but positive interest rate. Along this flat portion of the cash demand schedule, banks would be completely indifferent either to increases or decreases in their excess reserves. Monetary action to encourage bank lending and deposit creation was likened to "pushing on a string," and monetary action to reduce bank excess reserves was regarded as an innocuous measure that might forestall later inflation. On those grounds, the Federal Reserve doubled member bank reserve requirements between August 16, 1936, and May 1, 1937.

Evidence presented in this study suggests strongly that this liquidity trap interpretation of the behavior of banks in the Great Depression should be rejected. If at low interest rates, banks in the 1930's became indifferent about the level of their excess reserve ratios, the doubling of member bank reserve requirements in 1936–37 would not have altered the level of the *total* reserve ratio for country member banks relative to the total reserve ratio for non-member banks. In fact, however, country member banks increased their ratio of total reserves to deposits, relative to that for non-members, by almost precisely the amount needed to restore their *excess* reserve ratio to the same relation with non-member banks' excess reserve ratio as existed before the reserve requirement increase. The liquidity trap hypothesis cannot explain why excess reserve ratios of Canadian banks did not increase during the 1930's in a manner similar to excess reserve ratios of U.S. banks. The pattern of fluctuation in Canadian interest rates and business activity during the 1930's paralleled that of the U.S. with sufficient fidelity to suggest that a liquidity trap should have arisen in both banking systems. Elasticity estimates also fail to confirm the liquidity trap hypothesis. If the banks' demand for excess cash becomes "absolute" at low interest rates, then at the very least there should be clear evidence that the interest elasticity of demand for excess cash as a percentage of deposits increases as the interest rate declines. Yet, the findings were by no means so clear-cut. About half the tests show increasing elasticity at progressively lower interest rates, whereas the other half show just the opposite.

SHIFTS IN LIQUIDITY PREFERENCES

The inadequacy of the liquidity trap interpretation of bank excess reserves in the 1930's prompted an extended examination of alternative hypotheses. The most fruitful of these turned out to be a fundamental element in existing theory of the individual banking firm. A bank that maximizes expected profits should gear its demand for excess cash to its expected cash drains. For given net yields on other assets and penalty costs of cash deficiencies, the larger the bank's expected imminent loss of cash, the larger should be its precautionary holdings of cash assets. During and after a bank liquidity crisis, for example, it would be natural for banks to fear inordinately large cash drains and to attempt as best they could to accumulate cash in sufficient amount to survive expected drains. Casual observation tends to support this connection between panics and bank cash; historically, the excess reserve ratios of U.S. banks have reached their highest levels in the aftermath of bank panics. Every bank crisis since 1874 has been followed by a rapid increase in excess reserve ratios. The implication of this pattern and the banking theory that explains it is that after panics the liquidity preference schedules of banks shifted drastically in the direction of greater desired cash holdings for given interest rates than would have been wanted in the absence of the banking trauma.

The principal alternative to the liquidity trap, then, is a shift hypothesis that links major and sharp shifts in the banking system's demand for cash to the anxieties produced by banking liquidity crises. There are several transition mechanisms by which the shifts might conceivably have worked themselves out. Two such mechanisms are explored in this study: these have been labeled the "shock" effect and the "inertia" effect. The shock effect envisages an immediate and abrupt shift to a much higher *desired* cash ratio at the crisis point, but a slow adjustment of the actual to the desired ratio. Gradually the cash ratio increases until an equilibrium of desired and actual cash is reached, after which the actual cash ratio declines as the shock effect on the desired cash ratio wears off. The inertia effect views the postcrisis shifts in desired and actual cash ratios as depending directly on a variable explicitly designed to represent expected cash drains: transitory deposit potential. A liquidity crisis will induce banks to be more cautious in estimating their permanent deposit creating potential, i.e., the maximum volume of reserves (corrected for the level of reserve requirements), which can be safely used to support deposits without risking a costly scramble for liquidity. In the aftermath of banking crises, banks tend rapidly to acquire substantial reserve balances owing to factors that are beyond the banks' direct control—notably gold inflows from abroad, return flows of currency from the public and actions of the monetary authority to increase bank reserves. But the liquidity crisis teaches banks to go very slowly in putting the new reserves to work—to regard them largely as transitory rather than permanent additions to their deposit-creating potential. Consequently, these new reserves find their way into the excess reserves of the banking system, whereas under ordinary calmer conditions they would be quickly converted into required reserves by the process of multiple deposit expansion.

The inertia and shock effect mechanisms are, of course, not mutually exclusive. In reality both may be at work, and in a more comprehensive framework of transitional adjustment, both might play a role. But our examination of the two mechanisms, viewing them separately as special cases of a more general shift hypothesis, suggests the rather clear-cut superiority of the inertia effect. The shock effect regression model fails entirely to explain variations in the New York banks' excess reserve ratio after the 1907 panic and is less effective than the inertia model in predicting fluctuations in the New York banks' excess reserve ratio during the 1930's. The shock effect explanation fails because it assigns insufficient importance to the postcrisis increase in bank reserves (or potential deposits). After the 1907 crisis, the influx of reserves to New York banks was relatively modest, and so was the increase in their excess reserve ratio— although the severity of the crisis would have suggested a drastic shock-induced increase in this ratio. In the 1930's, the two peaks in New York banks' excess reserve ratio each occurred three years after the presumed crisis points—a much longer lag than the shock effect would have suggested from previous experience. Yet these peaks correspond closely in timing with the peaks in potential deposits.

Under the inertia explanation, the high postcrisis correlations of excess reserve ratios and current potential deposits are readily explainable as due to the large transitory component of potential deposits at such times. This transitory component is caused by a lengthening of the memory period that banks employ in estimating their permanent deposit potential. The crisis intensifies the inertia or caution with which banks revise their expectations in the light of new experience. As current potential deposits expand after crises, transitory potential deposits (or expected cash drain) grow large. As the transitory component in current potential deposits grows, banks hold more excess reserves in anticipation of larger cash drains. The inertia effect also manifests itself in longer postcrisis lags of growth in actual deposits behind growth in current potential deposits than would occur under normal banking conditions. Expansion of earning assets proceeds along with the deposit expansion. Among different asset categories, the lag in response to growth in lending capacity is greatest for business loans, least for highly liquid short-term money market assets.

Like the shock effect, the inertia effect also gradually wears off after enough time has elapsed from a previous crisis. This is revealed by the pattern of variation in estimates of β, the expectations or "memory" coefficient for permanent deposit potential. Following each crisis, the estimated value of β declines (i.e., the memory period lengthens) but later returns to normal levels. This regular pattern to the variation in β is a most striking empirical finding and invites further investigation. While the evidence is not conclusive, it suggests that a promising line of inquiry would be to attempt to establish a functional relation between the crisis shock and the expectations lag. Such a model might well be capable of explaining a large proportion of the variance in excess reserve ratios left unexplained by the simple inertia model used in this study.

A Postmortem on Pushing on a String

Does a finding that banks respond with a very long lag to changes in their reserves or deposit-creating potential imply that the monetary authority would be powerless to influence the volume of derivative deposits that banks create? I think not. So long as changes in the current level of expected potential deposits have any effect at all in changing the level of expected potential deposits to which banks, by hypothesis, respond, it is possible to induce expansion or contraction of bank earning assets and derivative deposits by means of the ordinary implements of monetary policy. The longer the lag, of course, the larger will open market operations or reserve requirement changes have to be to effect a given immediate change in actual derivative deposits. On the other hand the ultimate impact on such deposits of a given once-and-for-all change in deposit potential will be of the same magnitude no matter what the lag. Consequently, the attempt to achieve the same immediate impact when the lag in response is long as when it is short, will carry with it a longer chain of reactions, having potentially greater total impact on derivative deposits, unless offsetting reductions in potential deposits are made by the monetary authority as the chain of reactions progresses.

Faced in the middle and late 1930's with a long lag in bank response to changes in their deposit-creating potential, the Federal Reserve authorities could, with considerable justification, regard the injection of additional reserves through open-market operations as storing up a reservoir of credit expansion that would very likely be tapped in the future. But the proper policy, in view of the high level of unemployment that still existed in 1936 and 1937, would have been to allow reserves to continue to climb through gold inflows, and to reinforce this by vigorous open-market purchases of government securities. When and if full employment were reattained, and it became necessary to brake the further rapid expansion of deposits, the reservoir of potential deposits that had been previously accumulated could have been reduced by open-market sales, gold sterilization, reserve requirement increases and the like. If, in the interim before full employment had been attained, the expectations lag of banks were to shorten, this should occasion no alarm on the part of the monetary authorities, for the shortening of the lag would have tended, in itself, to reduce the size of the reservoir of deposit-creating ability, and thereby ease the task of applying the brakes. The magnitude of the tightening measures—the dollar amount of open-market sales, for example—could be smaller because of this and because a given dollar amount of reduction in current potential deposits would have a larger immediate impact, when lags in response are short, than when they are long.

APPENDIX A

Stock-Flow Model of the Demand for Bank Cash

E<small>QUATION</small> (2.10) of the text may be regarded as the special case of (2.11) in which the demand for cash is in full equilibrium.[1] there will be no incentive to change ρ at a position of full equilibrium, so that $\dot{\rho}$ will be zero. In general, however, ρ will be either positive or negative; positive values of $\dot{\rho}$ will tend to be associated with an excess of full equilibrium over actual ρ, while negative values of $\dot{\rho}$ will be associated with an excess of actual ρ over full equilibrium ρ. Or to turn the thing around, if actual ρ falls short of full equilibrium ρ, banks will attempt to increase ρ, that is attempt to attain a positive rate of change $\dot{\rho} > 0$, and conversely. It is usual to reserve for full equilibrium positions the term "desired," but for any given instant, the bank would be willing to hold any actual amount of cash, provided that it can attain the rate of change in cash at which it desires to approach full equilibrium.[2]

To a linear approximation, at a position of full equilibrium (i.e., where desired and actual cash are equal), (2.11) can be written

$$\rho^\circ = a_1 + a_2 r + a_3 d + \ldots + a_7 q , \qquad (A.1)$$

where ρ° symbolizes desired cash.

If the bank is out of full equilibrium, the rate at which it will attempt to change the cash ratio is a monotonic increasing function of the difference between the desired and the actual cash ratio:

$$\dot{\rho} = h(\rho^\circ - \rho) . \qquad (A.2)$$

[1] The notion of "full equilibrium" is analogous to the stationary state concept of the marginal productivity of capital in the model in which the particular variant of stock-flow analysis used here was apparently first introduced. See the article entitled "Capital, Investment and Interest," in A. P. Lerner, *Essays in Economic Analysis* (London: Macmillan & Co., 1953), pp. 347–53. Also see M. Friedman, *Price Theory—a Provisional Text* (Chicago: Aldine, 1962), pp. 246–63.

[2] It is an implicit assumption in these stock-flow models that the desired rate of change always equals the actual rate of change.

Expanding (A.2) around a position of full equilibrium, we get:

$$\dot{\rho} = h(0) + h'(0)[(\rho^\circ - \rho) - 0] + \cdots$$
$$= \epsilon(\rho^\circ - \rho) . \tag{A.3}$$

Substituting (A.1) in (A.3), we get a demand equation in terms of observable variables,

$$\rho = a_1 + a_2 r + a_3 d + \ldots + a_7 q - \frac{1}{\epsilon} \dot{\rho} . \tag{A.4}$$

This stock-flow adjustment model is often stated in difference equation form. Replacing $\dot{\rho}$ by $\rho_t - \rho_{t-1}$, (A.3) becomes

$$\rho_t - \rho_{t-1} = \gamma(\rho_{t-1}^\circ - \rho_{t-1}) + \theta(\rho_t^\circ - \rho_{t-1}^\circ) , \tag{A.5}$$

where two terms are now necessary to express the prospect that, in general, to the extent that the change in the actual cash ratio from $t - 1$ to t is controlled by the bank, the change in cash will be comprised of two different adjustments representing the attempt by the bank in the period between $t - 1$ and t to (a) close the gap between desired and actual cash that existed at the outset of the period and (b) to close the gap between desired cash at the end of the period and desired cash at the beginning of the period.[3] In the special case in which $\gamma = \theta$, (A.5) reduces to

$$\rho_t - \rho_{t-1} = \gamma(\rho_t^\circ - \rho_{t-1}) , \tag{A.6}$$

which is the usual form used in empirical applications.[4]

Dating the variables in (A.1) and substituting in (A.5), we obtain the following demand equation in terms of observables:

$$\rho_t = \gamma a_1 + \theta a_2 r_t + \theta a_3 d_t + \ldots + \theta a_7 q_t + (\gamma - \theta) a_2 r_{t-1}$$
$$+ (\gamma - \theta) a_3 d_{t-1} + \ldots + (\gamma - \theta) a_7 q_{t-1} + (1 - \gamma) \rho_{t-1} . \tag{A.7}$$

Except in two special cases, (a) where all but one of the variables in (A.1) drop out, or (b) where $\gamma = \theta$, the fitting of (A.7) will not yield unique estimates of the structural parameters $\gamma, \theta, a_1, a_2, \ldots, a_7$ except by iterative procedures.[5]

[3] This general formation of the adjustment equation is due to Professor Milton Friedman.

[4] M. Nerlove, *Distributed Lags and Demand Analysis for Agricultural and Other Commodities*, U.S. Department of Agriculture Handbook No. 141 (Washington: U.S. Government Printing Office, 1958).

[5] For example, Taylor's series expansion of (A.7) around arbitrary initial values of the parameters will linearize (A.7) in terms of increments to the parameters. Fitting of the linearized equation will then yield estimates of the increments required to modify the arbitrary initial values before proceeding to a second stage of approximation.

Apart from the mechanics of stock-flow relationships, it is, of course, a moot question whether banks can usefully be regarded as "off" their full equilibrium demand curve for cash. The answer depends mainly on how closely spaced in time our observations are in comparison with the length of time banks take to make the adjustments necessary to restore themselves to full equilibrium. Unless we are prepared to view these adjustments as literally instantaneous, the question must be decided on the basis of empirical findings. In principle, a change in any of the parameters in (2.10) or in any variable influencing bank demand for cash which has been omitted from (2.10) can throw banks out of full equilibrium.

The stock-flow model just outlined represents another stage of simplification—this time, of the general theory of investment decision over time.[6] In a fuller treatment it would be desirable to derive the adjustment equation from principles of inter-temporal utility optimization. For the present purposes, it is sufficient to follow the usual practice of appending the stock-flow relation to the static or full equilibrium model, without justification of lagged responses in terms of opportunities and preferences.

[6] J. Hirshleifer, "On the Theory of Optimal Investment Decision," *Journal of Political Economy*, LXVI (August, 1958), 329–52, and M. J. Bailey, "Formal Criteria for Investment Decisions," *Journal of Political Economy*, LXVII (October, 1959), 476–88. R. Eisner and R. Strotz, "Determinants of Business Investment," in *Impacts of Monetary Policy*, a Series of Research Studies Prepared for the Commission on Money and Credit (Englewood Cliffs, N.J.: Prentice-Hall, Inc., 1964), pp. 60–337.

APPENDIX B

Detailed Description of Variables Used in Chapter VII and Appendix D

THIS APPENDIX contains more complete definitions of the variables employed in the regressions and correlations of Chapter VII and Appendix D. Because of their importance to the study, special attention is given to explaining the methods of estimating the inertia effect variable, transitory potential deposits (q_t), and the shock effect variable (A_t).

THE VARIABLES

A. Excess Reserve Ratio

ρ_{et} = excess reserves[1] as a percentage of net deposits subject to reserve requirements (less required reserves) plus U.S. government deposits in periods when such deposits were not subject to reserve requirements, New York City weekly reporting banks 1919–55. Monthly averages of Wednesday figures (Friday figures, through April, 1921).[2]

[1] Excess reserves are estimates derived by applying required reserve percentages to time and net demand deposits subject to reserve. The estimates are only approximate because member banks are permitted to calculate required reserves on the basis of their average time and net demand deposits over a "reserve period." For New York banks, this reserve period was one week, beginning with October 1, 1919, except for the period January 1, 1928, to February 28, 1942, during which required reserves were computed for semiweekly periods. Monthly averages of daily figures for central reserve city banks in New York City might reduce the error in estimating excess reserves but are not available for the period prior to January, 1929, and are not strictly comparable in coverage of banks to the weekly reporting series. One advantage of the weekly reporting series is that an attempt was made to preserve continuity by avoiding spurious changes in the sample coverage.

[2] Seasonally adjusted except where otherwise noted in the tables that follow. The seasonal adjustment procedures used throughout were U.S. Census Bureau Method II programed for the Univac I computer and an adaptation of the Census Method II programed at the Federal Reserve Board for the IBM 650 computer. Both procedures involve calculating ratios to moving averages to derive seasonal factors. The programs require that the series to be seasonally adjusted consist of positive numbers. Since the excess reserve percentage is sometimes negative, it was decided to add an arbitrary 100 per cent to all excess reserve or excess cash reserve figures before seasonal adjustment. This rather unsatisfactory adjustment was dictated by the unavailability of a seasonal adjustment computer program based on arithmetic differences from moving averages.

122

B. *Excess Cash Reserve Ratio*

ρ_t = excess reserves plus vault cash as a percentage of net deposits subject to reserve requirements (less required reserves) plus U.S. government deposits, in periods when such deposits were not subject to reserve requirements, New York City weekly reporting banks. Monthly averages of Wednesday figures (Friday figures, through April, 1921).[3]

= excess cash reserves (specie and legal tender plus 5 per cent redemption fund less the 25 per cent required reserves against net deposits) as a percentage of net deposits subject to reserve requirements (less required reserves), New York Clearing House member banks 1874–1913. Monthly series represent averages of daily figures for the week nearest to mid-month.[4]

C. *Cost of Holding Excess Reserves*

r_t = call money (renewal) rate, New York Stock Exchange, August, 1874–December, 1929.[5]

= average yield on U.S. Treasury short-term obligations, January, 1930–December, 1955, adjusted to a taxable equivalent yield basis for the period prior to March, 1941, when these obligations became fully taxable. For January–December, 1930, represents yield on three- to six-month Treasury notes and certificates. For January, 1931–December, 1933 is the unweighted average of the yield on three- to six-month Treasury notes and certificates and of the yield on Treasury bills (new issues), except for October and November, 1932, when the former yield was negative, and the yield on Treasury bills alone was used. For January, 1934, to February, 1941 is the unweighted average of yields on Treasury bills (new issues) and dealers' bid quotations on three-month Treasury bills, except in January, March, October, and November, 1940, and January, 1941, when new issue yields were negative and the dealers' quoted yield alone was used. For March, 1941, to March, 1942 is the yield on Treasury bills (new issues). For April, 1942, to December, 1955, is a weighted average of yields on Treasury bills (new issues) and certificates (nine to twelve months). The weights are the proportions of bills and of certificates that were held by all member banks, linearly interpolated from call report dates.[6]

D. *Risk Premium or Expected Probability of Default on Lower-Grade Corporate Bonds*

P_t^a = arithmetic spread between Macaulay's unadjusted railroad bond yield and his adjusted railroad bond yield, August,

[3] *Ibid.*   [4] *Ibid.*   [5] *Ibid.*   [6] *Ibid.*

1874–December, 1929. After 1929, the value of this series is taken to be zero.[7]

σ_t = cumulated product of the slopes of the regression lines which minimize the sum of squares of the orthogonal distances of observations from the regression line, where the observations are the logarithms of the yields on individual railroad bond issues in month t and month $t - 1$. Macaulay calls this regression line a "sigma" line and the slope of the sigma line represents the ratio of the standard deviation of the logarithms of bond yields in month t to the standard deviation of the logarithms of bond yields in month $t - 1$. By means of the sigma lines, Macaulay constructs a "drift"-free index number of the yield of railroad bonds, which is then used to adjust the unadjusted index of railroad bond yields to remove longtime economic drift. See Macaulay.[8] The cumulated product of the sigma slopes may be regarded as an index of changes in the relative dispersion in grade of corporate bonds, which is one way to measure changes in "drift" or risk premia on bonds. The series covers the period August, 1874, to December, 1929, and is not seasonally adjusted. For the period August, 1874, to December, 1878, monthly values were interpolated from quarterly estimates.[9]

P_t^m = arithmetic spread between yields on Moody's Baa and Aaa corporate bonds, 1919–55.[10]

E. *Liquidity Premium or Expected Capital Gain (or Loss) from Holding Long-Term Investments*

$B_t - S_t$ = arithmetic spread between long-term and short-term interest rates, 1874–1913, 1919–55.

B_t = Macaulay's unadjusted railroad bond yield, August, 1874–December, 1913.[11]

= Macaulay's adjusted railroad bond yield, 1919–December, 1930.[12]

= U.S. Treasury long-term, partially taxable bonds, January, 1931–February, 1941.[13]

= U.S. Treasury long-term fully taxable bonds, March, 1941–December, 1955.[14]

[7] Not seasonally adjusted.

[8] F. R. Macaulay, *The Movements of Interest Rates, Bond Yields and Stock Prices in the United States since 1856* (New York: National Bureau of Economic Research, 1938), pp. 97–123, A115–29.

[9] Not seasonally adjusted.

[10] *Ibid.*

[11] *Ibid.*

[12] *Ibid.*

[13] *Ibid.*

[14] *Ibid.*

S_t = Macaulay's commercial paper rate in New York City on choice 60–90 day two name paper, August, 1874–December, 1913.[15]

= Macaulay's rate on 90-day prime bankers' acceptances in New York City 1919–December, 1930.[16]

= U.S. Treasury bill rate, new issues, January, 1931–January, 1934.[17]

= U.S. Treasury bill rate, dealers' quotations, February, 1934–December, 1955.[18]

F. Penalty Rates

d_t = discount rate, New York Federal Reserve Bank, 1919–April, 1942, and August, 1947–December, 1955.[19]

= zero, May, 1942–July, 1947.

p_t = discount rate, New York Federal Reserve Bank, 1919–March, 1928, and January, 1932–April, 1942.[20]

= federal funds rate, New York City, April, 1928–December, 1931, and August, 1947–December, 1955.[21]

= zero, May, 1942–July, 1947.

G. Potential Deposits

Dp_t = total specie and legal tender ÷ .25 (the required reserve ratio), New York Clearing House member banks, August 1874–December, 1913.[22]

= total reserves and vault cash ÷ the average required reserve ratio against net deposits subject to reserve, January 1919–December, 1955.[23]

E_t = expected (or "permanent") deposit potential. Computed from current deposit potential (Dp_t) by methods described below.

q_t = transitory deposit potential.

= $[(Dp_t \div E_t) - 1] \times 100$.

H. Crisis Variable

A_t = a variable representing the combination of time from previous crisis and lagged response to the effect of crisis on desired cash. Discussed in detail below.

[15] See footnote 2, *supra*, p. 122.

[16] *Ibid.*

[17] *Ibid.*

[18] *Ibid.*

[19] Not seasonally adjusted.

[20] *Ibid.*

[21] *Ibid.*

[22] See footnote 2, *supra*, p. 122.

[23] *Ibid.*

I. Miscellaneous Variables

$\Delta\rho_t$ = rate of change in ρ_t.

$\quad = (\rho_{t+1} - \rho_{t-1})/2.$

T = a number representing time, increasing by increments of one each month, beginning with zero in June 1874, and ending with 977 in December, 1955.

0 or 1 = a dummy variable, taking the value of one in the period May, 1942 to August, 1947, and zero in all other months, 1919–December, 1955.

THE MEASUREMENT OF TRANSITORY POTENTIAL DEPOSITS

In Meigs's study of the demand by banks for free reserves, an important variable in explaining this demand is the current rate of change in unborrowed bank reserves (adjusted for changing reserve requirements).[24] This rate of change turns out to be positively correlated with the level of free reserves as a percentage of deposits, and Meigs interprets this result as reflecting a lag in response of banks to actions of the Federal Reserve whenever these actions have the instantaneous effect of dislodging banks from their "full equilibrium" desired free reserve ratio (the desired full equilibrium being defined as a function of interest rates at a zero rate of change in unborrowed reserves).

In terms of our banking model, the rate of change in unborrowed reserves can be viewed as one form in which the theoretical construct, expected cash drain, might be given an empirical counterpart: the faster unborrowed reserves are increasing, the larger the expected cash drain would be for a given reserve aggregate, and conversely if unborrowed reserves are decreasing. But stating the relation between the rate of change in unborrowed reserves and expected cash drain in this way reveals an obvious defect; eventually banks may become so accustomed to an average rate of growth in unborrowed reserves that they no longer expect cash drain because of such growth, and therefore do not desire to hold a higher free reserve ratio than they would if the expected average rate of growth were zero.

This is a matter of secondary importance, however; the statistical bias introduced by this factor is most likely to affect the estimate of the constant term in regressions where the free reserve ratio is dependent. On the presumption that banks expect a constant secular rate of growth in unborrowed reserves, Meigs's procedure is equivalent to measuring the rates of change as deviations from zero rather than from this constant expected

[24] A. James Meigs, *Free Reserves and the Money Supply* (Chicago: University of Chicago, 1962).

rate of growth in unborrowed reserves. Consequently, the regression constant would be biased downward by some unknown amount, but regression slope estimates would be unaffected.

A more serious shortcoming of the current rate of change in unborrowed reserves variable is that it assumes that bankers have virtually no memory. What happened to unborrowed reserves last month or the month before has no effect on current banker decisions as to the desired level of the free reserve ratio. Now this may, in fact, be an accurate portrayal of the state of affairs,[25] but it would seem preferable to find some way of allowing the data themselves to suggest the appropriate "memory period."

An approach that now has some claim to being considered standard in empirical economic analysis is to assign exponentially declining weights to the current and past values of the series in question, in the manner prescribed by Cagan[26] and Friedman[27] in their studies of hyperinflation and consumption expenditures. The series, in our case, could be the current measured rate of change in total deposit potential[28] and the result of averaging a group of weighted current and past values of this series would be one of a set of possible time series representing the expected rate of change in total potential deposits. By use of different weighting patterns to generate alternative expected rates of change series and by successive substitution of one such series for another in the same regression model, it is possible to select—by goodness of fit criteria—the weighting pattern and expected rate of change series that best represent the "memory period" of bankers.

This is the procedure that will be followed, except that instead of the rate of change of potential deposits, we shall construct expected total potential deposit series, E_t, from a time series of current total potential deposits, Dp_t, and take as our measure of transitory potential deposits, q_t, the ratio $[(Dp_t/E_t) - 1] \times 100$. This way of deriving our transitory series has some advantages in terms of reducing the preliminary computational

[25] That such is not the case, is suggested by Meigs's finding that an average of the rates of change for the preceding month and the current month gave better results than the current month's rate of change alone. *Ibid.*, Chap. V.

[26] P. Cagan, "The Monetary Dynamics of Hyperinflation," in M. Friedman (ed.), *Studies in the Quantity Theory of Money* (Chicago: University of Chicago, 1956), pp. 37–47.

[27] M. Friedman, *A Theory of the Consumption Function* (New York: National Bureau of Economic Research, 1957), pp. 142–56.

[28] Potential deposits, as defined earlier (above, p. 125), seems well adapted to the long period investigation we have embarked on. For certain shorter periods, some other reserves concept—be it total reserves, unborrowed reserves, or total reserves less Federal Reserve float or total "available" reserves—might be more appropriate.

burden but also has an important drawback, which will be examined later on.

The expectations hypothesis underlying this approach is that expected potential deposits, E_t, is revised per unit of time at a rate that is a proportion, β, of the difference between current potential deposits, Dp_t, and expected potential deposits. Formally, this can be expressed as a differential equation.

$$\frac{dE_t}{dt} = \beta(Dp_t - E_t), \qquad (B.1)$$

which has the solution,

$$E_t = Ge^{-\beta t} + \beta \int_{-\infty}^{t} e^{\beta(T-t)} Dp_T dT. \qquad (B.2)$$

The constant term can be set equal to zero on the presumption that Dp_T and therefore E_t was zero before some distant date in the past. A trend component, a, can be incorporated by the following modification:

$$E_t = \beta \int_{-\infty}^{t} e^{(\beta-a)(T-t)} Dp_T dT.^{29} \qquad (B.3)$$

The first observed values of Dp_t were in September, 1873, and January, 1919. It was necessary to take a second starting point in 1919 because of differences between the Clearing House banks series and the weekly reporting series in coverage of banks. The assumed value of a was the same in both cases.

By inserting different values of β in the approximation formula for (B.3), a set of alternative E_t series were calculated, and from them, a set of alternative q_t, or transitory potential deposits, series as defined previously. The regressions reported are those which gave the highest R^2 among sets of regressions in which different β weighted q_t series were tested. The β value for each such series is also listed.

For any given values of a and β, a discrete approximation to (B.3) can be derived as follows:

$$E_t \approx \beta \sum_{\tau=-\infty}^{t} Dp_\tau \int_{\tau-1}^{\tau} e^{(\beta-a)(T-t)} dT$$

$$\approx \beta \sum_{\tau=-\infty}^{t} Dp_\tau \left\{ \frac{1}{\beta-a} \left[e^{(\beta-a)(\tau-t)} - e^{(\beta-a)(\tau-1-t)} \right] \right\}$$

$$\approx \frac{\beta}{\beta-a} \lim_{n\to\infty} \left\{ Dp_t(1 - e^{a-\beta}) + Dp_{t-1}(e^{a-\beta} - e^{2(a-\beta)}) + \cdots + Dp_{t-n}(e^{n(a-\beta)} - e^{(n+1)(a-\beta)}) \right\}$$

[29] The value of a was taken to be .0035 on the basis of preliminary examination of the Dp_t series.

$$\approx \frac{\beta}{\beta - a}(1 - e^{a-\beta})\,[\,Dp_t + Dp_{t-1}e^{a-\beta} + \,\ldots\, + Dp_{t-n}e^{n(\beta-a)}\,]$$

$$\approx \frac{\beta}{\beta - a}(1 - e^{a-\beta})\,Dp_t + e^{a-\beta}E_{t-1}\,.$$

The initial value of E_{t-1} (say E_0) is estimated by assuming that before $t = 0$, Dp_t increased at a constant rate, a, such that if Dp_0 is the first observed value,

$$Dp_{-t} = Dp_0(1 + a)^{-t}\,.$$

Consequently,

$$E_0 = \frac{\beta}{\beta - a}(1 - e^{a-\beta})\,[\,Dp_0 + Dp_{-1}e^{a-\beta} + Dp_{-n}e^{n(a-\beta)} + \,\ldots\,]$$

$$= \frac{\beta}{\beta - a}(1 - e^{a-\beta})\,(Dp_0)\left[1 + \frac{e^{a-\beta}}{1+a} + \,\ldots\, + \left(\frac{e^a\ \beta}{1+a}\right)^n + \ldots\right]$$

$$= \left[\frac{\beta(1 - e^{a-\beta})}{(\beta - a)\left(1 - \dfrac{e^{a-\beta}}{1+a}\right)}\right]Dp_0\,.$$

For another approximation see Cagan.[30] The general approach is closely related to that developed by L. H. Koyck.[31]

ESTIMATION OF THE SHOCK EFFECT VARIABLE

In previous chapters it was suggested that one immediate effect of a banking crisis may be to create an urge by banks to hold much higher excess reserve ratios than are customary under normal conditions. After the crisis is passed, banks might be expected to relax their caution only gradually by slowly reducing their desired excess reserve ratios. Then the desired level of the excess reserve ratio after banking crises may be, in part, a decreasing function of time elapsed from previous crisis.

Accordingly, the A_t variable is developed as follows. First, suppose that a demand equation that works fairly well under normal conditions takes the form

$$\hat{\rho}_t = a + b\,\log_e r_t + cP_t^a + dq_t\,, \tag{B.4}$$

where q_t represents the particular β weighted transitory potential deposits series which does the best job of predicting ρ_t.

[30] "The Monetary Dynamics of Hyperinflation," pp. 39–41.

[31] *Distributed Lags and Investment Analysis* (Amsterdam: North-Holland Publishing Co., 1954).

But a regression of a form such as (B.4), fitted to observations taken from "normal" periods, may not accurately predict the cash positions of banks during periods affected by banking crisis. If we let x_t denote this error of prediction,

$$x_t = \rho_t - \hat{\rho}_t . \tag{B.5}$$

The objective of the A_t variable is to test whether these x_t residuals are systematically related to time from crisis. Now, in the same way that $\hat{\rho}_t$ can be regarded as an estimate of desired ρ_t, under normal conditions, the x_t residuals may form a basis for estimating the desired addition to normal ρ_t arising because of crisis conditions. The desired addition might be represented by a linear function of an exponential transformation of time elapsed from previous crises. This may be written:

$$x_t^0 = \mu + \kappa \sum_{i=1}^{n} e^{\delta(t_i - t)} \tag{B.6}$$

$$= \mu + \kappa C_t ,$$

where the summation is over all previous crises, $i = 1$ to n, and where x_t^0 designates the desired additional excess cash reserve ratio, t_i is a crisis date previous to t, and μ, κ, and δ are parameters.

Under normal conditions, differences between desired and actual ρ_t may be negligible. But under the impact of crisis, this may not be the case; although banks want to hold more cash, they may find it difficult to achieve this objective quickly. If we assume that banks are only able to change x_t at a rate that is proportional to the difference between desired and actual x_t, we are supposing their behavior can be described by the following differential equation:

$$\frac{dx_t}{dt} = \pi (x_t^0 - x_t). \tag{B.7}$$

Substituting (B.6) in (B.7), we get

$$\frac{dx_t}{dt} = \pi [(\mu + \kappa C_t) - x_t] \tag{B.8}$$

$$= \pi\mu + \pi\kappa C_t - \pi x_t ,$$

which has the solution,

$$x_t = \mu + H e^{-\pi t} + \kappa\pi e^{-\pi t} \int_{-\infty}^{t} e^{\pi T} C_T dT \tag{B.9}$$

$$= \mu + H e^{-\pi t} + \kappa A_t .$$

For a point in time t^* sufficiently distant from a crisis date, it can be assumed that

$$\sum_{i=1}^{n} e^{\delta(t_i - t)} \approx 0$$

so that $x_{t^*}^0 \approx \mu$. If for this date, $x_t^{0*} - x_t^* \approx 0$ also,

$$x_{t^*} = \mu + He^{-\pi t^*} = \mu , \quad \text{and } He^{-\pi t^*} = 0 , \quad \text{so } H = 0 .$$

Therefore (B.9) can be written

$$x_t = \mu + \kappa A_t . \tag{B.10}$$

In fitting (B.10) by least-squares methods, a value of .04167 was preassigned to δ. This value of δ implies that $e^{\delta(t_i - t_n)} < .05\, e^{\delta(t_i - t)}$, where t_n denotes a date seventy-two months after the crisis date. Inspection of the residuals x_t indicated that the presumed crisis effect in all cases was virtually dissipated within six years after the crisis date.[32]

It can be shown that A_t can be approximated by the formula,

$$A_t = (1 - e^{-\pi})C_t + e^{-\pi}A_{t-1} , \tag{B.11}$$

provided a suitable initial value of A_{t-1} can be obtained, say, by choosing a point sufficiently distant from crisis such that A_{t-1} for that date can be assumed to be zero.

The estimation problem then boils down to choosing from among a set of alternative π-weighted A_t series, the series which maximizes R^2 in regressions of the form of (B.10).

[32] The preassignment of a value to δ is statistically inefficient, since it uses only part of the available information—the observations of x_t lying near the "tail-end" of the exponential decay function. But the procedure has the advantage of avoiding the fitting of a regression that is non-linear in the parameters.

APPENDIX C

Sources and Limitations of Data

THE SOURCES of data are listed in the order of appearance of the variables which are based upon them.

I. CHAPTER III

A. Table 2, page 49

Reserves, net deposits, time deposits, and vault cash for member banks were taken from U.S., Federal Reserve Board, *Member Bank Call Report* (Washington: Federal Reserve Board, June 30, 1927). Excess reserves were calculated by applying required reserve ratios to net demand deposits subject to reserve and time deposits for each reserve class of banks in each reserve district and subtracting from total reserves.

Deposits of all suspended commercial banks were from U.S., Board of Governors of the Federal Reserve System, *Banking and Monetary Statistics* (Washington: Federal Reserve, 1943), Table No. 67, p. 285. Deposits of all commercial banks were from U.S., Board of Governors of the Federal Reserve System, *All-Bank Statistics* (Washington: Federal Reserve Board, 1959), *passim.*

State population data: from U.S., Bureau of Census, *Census of Population: 1960*, I, Table No. 3, *passim.*

Airline distances: from C. A. Whitten, U.S. Coast and Geodetic Survey, Special Publication No. 238, *Airline Distances between Cities in the United States* (Washington: U.S. Government Printing Office, 1961), *passim.*

Earnings and total loans and investments of national banks from U.S., Comptroller of the Currency, *Annual Report, 1927* (Washington: U.S. Government Printing Office, 1928), pp. 535–36, 614–25. Earnings are the sum of interest and discount on loans and investments, profits on securities sold and recoveries on loans and investments, less losses and depreciation charged off on loans, discounts, bonds, securities, etc.

Interest on balances due from domestic banks, for national banks, from Comptroller of the Currency, *Annual Report, 1927*, pp. 614–25. Balances due from banks, for national banks, *ibid.*, pp. 535–36.

132

II. Chapter VI

A. Table 4, page 88

Specie, legal tender, national bank-note circulation, and net deposits subject to reserve requirements, New York Clearing House Banks, from A. P. Andrew, *Statistics for the United States, 1867–1909*, U.S., Congress, Senate, National Monetary Commission (Washington: U.S. Government Printing Office, 1910), Table No. 28, pp. 81–118; *Commercial and Financial Chronicle* (New York: William Dana Co., 1909–14), various issues. Excess reserve ratios are annual averages of daily figures for the week nearest mid-month.

Before July, 1874, excess reserves were calculated as total specie and legal tender less reserves required against circulation and net deposits; from July, 1874, excess reserves were calculated as total specie and legal tender, plus 5 per cent redemption fund, less reserves required against net deposits. Revised deposits represent net deposits less required reserves. Net deposits subject to reserve exclude Treasury deposits, for the May, 1908, to December, 1909, period, but these are apparently included in reporting figures for Clearing House banks thereafter. For the May, 1908, to December, 1909, period, reported Treasury deposits were counted as part of revised deposits; after December, 1909, the required reserve ratio was applied to the reported "net" deposit figure, although strictly speaking Treasury deposits should be excluded from this calculation. Judging from call reports of New York national banks, Treasury deposits were quite negligible after 1909. No attempt was made to adjust figures on specie and legal tenders or on bank deposits for the premium on gold during the preresumption period 1872–78.

Call loan renewal rate and commercial paper rate from F. B. Macaulay, *The Movements of Interest Rates, Bond Yields and Stock Prices in the United States since 1856* (New York: National Bureau of Economic Research, 1938), pp. A142–56. Annual averages of monthly figures.

Deposits or liabilities of all bank failures or suspensions are the sum of figures for suspended national banks and state and private banks. Figures for suspended national banks from Federal Deposit Insurance Corporation, *Annual Report* (Washington: U.S. Government Printing Office, 1934), pp. 92–93. Represents claims proved, 1872–80, and deposits, 1881–1914. Claims proved and deposits were practically identical in the period 1881–99. Figures exclude banks in voluntary liquidation, but include banks restored to solvency. Figures for private and state banks from Federal Deposit Insurance Corporation, *Annual Report, 1934*, and U.S., Comptroller of the Currency, *Annual Report, 1931* (Washington: U.S.

Government Printing Office, 1932) p. 1041. Represents liabilities of banks that did not reopen, 1872–99, liabilities or resources of private bank failures and suspended state banks, 1900–1914. Calendar years are presented as reported, 1872–95; reported figures are adjusted to a calendar year basis for 1896–1900 by taking weighted averages of figures for successive twelve-month periods ending August 31 (1897–99) and June 30 (1899–1900) on the assumption that failures were evenly distributed throughout the year. The figure for 1899 is based on liabilities (mislabeled "deposits") of state and private bank failures (mislabeled "suspensions") for 1899 and 1900 as reported in the Comptroller's *Annual Report*. All other figures are presented as reported in the aforementioned F.D.I.C. *Annual Report*, except for private bank failures, 1900–1914, which are adjusted to a calendar year basis from reported figures on a year-ended-June 30 basis. It should be noted that the 1900–1914 figures for liabilities or resources of suspended state banks are an amalgam of data from H. Parker Willis, "The Banking Inquiry of 1925" (unpublished study on file at the School of Business, Columbia University), and from Bradstreet's reports to the Comptroller of the Currency. The Willis data are on a calendar-year basis, and account for about 85 per cent of the total reported resources or liabilities. The Bradstreet data refer to years ended on June 30.

Total deposits of the Treasury and the public from M. Friedman and A. Schwartz, *A Monetary History of the United States, 1867–1960* (Princeton, N.J.: Princeton University Press for the National Bureau of Economic Research, 1963). Represents total deposits adjusted of commercial banks plus government deposits, as of June 30 of each year. In the earlier years, where June 30 estimates were not available, they were derived by linear interpolation from seasonally adjusted figures for dates nearest June 30.

Total deposits of national banks: from Comptroller of the Currency, *Annual Reports*, various years, 1872–1913.

Liabilities of business failures from U.S. Bureau of the Census, *Historical Statistics of the United States* (Washington: U.S. Government Printing Office, 1960), product of Series Nos. V1 and V3, p. 570.

Net national product based on unpublished estimates by S. Kuznets, but were increased by certain percentages to correspond, roughly, to Kendrick's adjustment of Kuznets' estimates to the Commerce Department definitions, as presented in *Historical Statistics of the United States*, Series No. F6, p. 139. The percentages were: 1872–96, 5 per cent; 1897–1901, 5.3 per cent; 1902–6, 4.2 per cent; 1907–11, 6.3 per cent; 1912–14, 6.6 per cent.

Dates of crises were taken to be: September, 1873; May, 1884; August, 1893; and October, 1907.

III. CHAPTER VII

A. Excess Reserve Ratio and Excess Cash Reserve Ratio, page 92

Total reserves, vault cash, U.S. government deposits and time and net demand deposits subject to reserve for the period 1919–55 were taken from *Banking and Monetary Statistics*, Table No. 49, pp. 164–95, and *Federal Reserve Bulletin* (Washington: U.S. Government Printing Office, 1942–46), various issues. Prior to August 23, 1935, net demand deposits consist of deposits of individuals, corporations, etc., and state and local governments, plus certified checks outstanding, plus foreign interbank deposits, plus the excess of due to domestic banks over the sum of balances due from domestic banks and cash items in process of collection. Between August 23, 1935, and April 13, 1943, net demand deposits included U.S. government demand deposits. Since August 23, 1935, the sum of balances due from domestic banks and cash items in process of collection have been subtracted from gross demand deposits subject to reserve rather than from balances due from domestic banks in computing net demand deposits. Between April 13, 1943, and June 30, 1947, U.S. government war loan and Series E bond accounts were exempt from reserve requirements. For purposes of calculating net demand deposits, total U.S. government demand deposits were subtracted from gross demand deposits, although this is only an approximate measure of war loan and Series E bond accounts. Subsequent to June 30, 1947, all U.S. government deposits have been subject to reserve requirements. Required reserves were estimated by applying the required reserve ratios against time and net demand deposits to the corresponding monthly averages of Wednesday figures for time and net demand deposits. When reserve requirements were changed during a given month, the required reserves for the month were estimated as weighted averages of required reserves under the old and under the new requirements, with the weights determined by the proportions of the month for which the respective reserve requirements were in force.

Specie, legal tender, national bank note circulation, and net deposits subject to reserve requirements were taken from the same sources as for Table 4 (see *supra*). Computation of the excess cash reserve ratio is the same as indicated in Table 4 except that Treasury deposits were not counted as part of revised deposits in the period, May, 1908, to December, 1909. This exclusion has a negligible effect on the excess reserve ratio.

B. *Short-Term Money Market Interest Rates, page 92*

Call money (renewal) rate from F. B. Macaulay, *op. cit.*, pp. A142–60. Yields on U.S. Treasury bills (new issues and dealers' quotations), three- to six-month Treasury notes and certificates, and nine- to twelve-month Treasury certificates from *Banking and Monetary Statistics*, Table No. 122, p. 460, and *Federal Reserve Bulletin*, 1942–56, various issues. Taxable equivalent yields were computed by dividing the reported yield by $1 - T$, where T is the rate of normal corporation income tax at the $25,000 level of taxable net income as given in Commerce Clearing House, *Standard Federal Tax Reports* (Chicago: Commerce Clearing House, 1960), p. 153.

C. *Potential Deposits, page 92*

Underlying data on specie and legal tender and total reserves plus vault cash are taken from same sources as in III. A (*supra*). There are certain imperfections in the data, however, to which the potential deposits estimates are particularly sensitive. These imperfections arise from the fact that the sample of banks comprising members of the New York Clearing House Association or weekly reporting member banks in New York City did not remain constant, owing to mergers, liquidations, dropouts, and additions. Such changes in sample composition introduce disturbances to the current values of potential deposits that, from the point of view of estimating expected potential deposits, are spurious, since there is no reason to expect the desired excess reserve ratio of a large group of banks to be systematically affected by the arbitrary addition to or subtraction from the group of one or more banks.

A chronological examination of the lists of members of the Clearing House Association given in the *Commercial and Financial Chronicle* disclosed that in the period between August, 1873, and December, 1913, there were forty-eight months in which new banks were admitted to membership (either by application or merger with members) or member banks were dropped through failure, suspension, or voluntary liquidation. There were undoubtedly other months in which members merged with non-members but which were not reported in the *Chronicle* because no change in bank name occurred. It was not found possible to trace these down. The majority of the traceable changes involved banks whose deposits were negligible compared with the total of deposits for all Clearing House banks. In six of the forty-eight months, however, the changes involved banks whose deposits amounted to more than 1 per cent of total Clearing House members' deposits; the largest such changes were in July, 1894, when two banks, with aggregate deposits amounting to 1.9 per cent of all Clearing House bank deposits, were added, and in January, 1908, when four banks that had failed during the banking crisis of 1907 did not reappear on the first published list of Clearing House members after the crisis. These banks had deposits, at latest report, totaling 1.8 per cent of all Clearing House bank deposits in January, 1908.

No attempt was made to adjust the reported Clearing House figures for these changes in the sample banks, inasmuch as they were very small and very numerous. The biases produced by the neglect of these changes in sample are believed to be relatively minor, inasmuch as the movements they introduce are much smaller than the average month-to-month percentage movements of current potential deposits during this period. The biases will be of two sorts. First, since most of the changes entailed the addition of new banks to membership, the estimated trend in expected deposit potential will be biased upward slightly. Actual potential deposits will also be biased upward on average by about the same percentage. If the changes had been perfectly smooth and continuous in occurrence, the two biases would offset each other in the calculations of transitory reserves. But to the extent that the changes occur in discrete jumps, transitory reserves will show spurious movements that will not be systematically related to the excess cash reserve ratio. This will have the effect of introducing a downward bias in the estimate of the best β weighted q_t series, as determined by our regressions and correlations.

The weekly reporting member bank series for New York banks is relatively free of this source of bias, at least for the period that has been dealt with in this study. Whenever a bank dropped out of the sample, for reasons other than merger with another weekly reporting bank, an attempt was made to replace it with another bank of approximately equal size and similar characteristics in other respects. By 1949, however, the availability of outside member banks suitable for this purpose had been greatly curtailed, and the practice was discontinued. Since then comparability of the series over time spans of more than a few years has also been hampered by periodic revisions of the sample banks. One such revision occurred in January, 1952, and has been mentioned previously. Another occurred in July, 1946, when the number of reporting banks was substantially increased. An overlap period, July, 1946–June, 1947, during which the weekly reporting data were reported on both the new and the old sample basis, permitted the adjustment of the figures on the new series basis to old series levels, by applying the ratio $x = A/B$, where A is the old series and B is the new series (averages for the overlap period), to the new series. The adjustment was confined to revising the series for total potential deposits, however, since it was determined that the change in the excess reserve ratio would be negligible, inasmuch as the change in the sample size affected total reserves, required reserves, and deposits in about equal proportion.

Aside from changes in sample size, there are limitations on the weekly reporting bank data arising from the fact that some of the smaller reporting banks were not subject to central reserve city reserve requirements, as assumed in this study. Moreover, certain of the reporting banks experienced changes in reserve classification as a result of mergers with other reporting banks and changes in the Federal Reserve's standards for determining reserve classification. Unfortunately, at this late date, the information that is needed to evaluate the degree of error caused by these peculiarities of the weekly reporting series is no longer available in Federal Reserve records.

D. Risk Premium or Expected Probability of Default on Lower-Grade Corporate Bonds, pages 92 and 123

Yields on Moody's Aaa and Baa corporate bonds from *Banking and Monetary Statistics*, Table No. 128, pp. 468–71, and *Federal Reserve Bulletin*, 1942–56, various issues.

Macaulay's unadjusted and adjusted railroad bond yields and cumulated product of "sigma" slopes from F. B. Macaulay, *op. cit.*, pp. A142–60, A115–29.

E. Spread between Long-Term and Short-Term Interest Rates, Page 124

Yields on U.S. Treasury long-term, partially taxable bonds from *Banking and Monetary Statistics*, Table No. 128, pp. 468–71.

Yields on U.S. Treasury long-term, fully taxable bonds from records of the Board of Governors of the Federal Reserve System.

Rates on commercial paper and bankers' acceptances from Macaulay, *op. cit.*, pp. A146–56, A251.

Treasury bill rates, new issues, from *Banking and Monetary Statistics*, Table No. 122, p. 460.

Treasury bill rates, dealers' quotations from *Banking and Monetary Statistics*, Table No. 122, p. 460, and records of the Board of Governors of the Federal Reserve System.

F. Penalty Rates, page 125

Discount rate on eligible paper, New York Federal Reserve Bank, from *Banking and Monetary Statistics*, Table No. 115, p. 442, and *Federal Reserve Bulletin*, 1942–56, various issues.

Federal funds rate: April, 1928, to July, 1931, monthly averages of weekly figures read from chart in B. H. Beckhart and J. G. Smith, *The New York Money Market* (New York: Columbia University Press, 1932), II, 47; August, 1931, to December, 1931, and August, 1947, to December, 1949, monthly averages of mid-points of Tuesday high and low quotes, from *New York Herald Tribune*, 1931 and 1947–49, various issues; January, 1950, to December, 1955, monthly averages of daily figures, from Garvin, Bantel and Co., New York (the principal broker in federal funds during the period in question).

APPENDIX D

Additional Regression Tests[1]

THREE BASIC MODELS are used in these tests. The first is a full equilibrium model of essentially the same type as (2.10) (*supra*) in that the desired and actual cash are taken to be equal at all observed points.[2] The second is designed to test for discrepancies between desired and actual cash by introduction of $\Delta\rho_t$, in the manner of (2.11). The third model employs the usual reduced form equation for testing for discrepancies between desired and actual quantities, i.e., an equation in which the lagged dependent variable appears as an independent variable, as in special case (*b*) of (A.7).

A. Tests on Clearing House Banks,
Table 10

The results of tests on monthly data from September, 1874, to November, 1913, are shown in Table 10. Equations (D.1)–(D.6) (Table 10) are designed to determine the relative explanatory power of $1/r_t$ and $\log_e r_t$ on the one hand and σ_t, P_t^a, and T, on the other. The results can be summed up by saying that $1/r_t$ works better than $\log_e r_t$, while P_t^a works better than either σ_t or T, although all of these variables appear to be highly significant and of the right sign. Other findings reported in Table 10 include the non-significance of the spread between long and short rates[3] and the consistently wrong but statistically significant sign of $\Delta\rho_t$. The spread between long and short rates might have been more successful if

[1] For a complete list and definitions of variables used in this Appendix, see Appendix B.

[2] In the reported regressions, cash position (ρ_t or ρ_{e_t}) is always dependent. Some experiments with interest rates dependent were unsuccessful in the sense that they produced rather low values of R^2 and structural coefficients having the wrong sign. The results can be rationalized on the grounds that the ρ_t and ρ_{e_t} series contain substantially larger errors of observation than the interest rate variable—a not implausible presumption.

Two other regression models were tested extensively on normal periods. One involved regressing ρ_t on ρ_{t-1}, $\log_e r_t$, P_t^a, and q_t.

[3] Equations (D.1), (D.2), (D.5), and (D.6) do, indeed, show $B_t - S_t$ to be significant, but show lower R^2 values than (D.3) and (D.4), where $B_t - S_t$ is not significant.

TABLE 10
REGRESSIONS, NEW YORK CLEARING HOUSE BANKS, 1874-1913[a]
(Monthly Data)

EQUATION NUMBER	TIME PERIOD COVERED	NUMBER OF OBSERVATIONS	CONSTANT TERM	COEFFICIENTS, STANDARD ERRORS (IN PARENTHESES) OF INDEPENDENT VARIABLES, AND β VALUES OF q_t VARIABLES (IN BRACKETS)										R^2
				$1/r_t$	$\log_e r_t$	q_t	ρ_{t-1}	$\log_e (Dp_{t+1}/Dp_{t-1})$	B_t-S_t	σ_t	P_i^a	$\Delta\rho_t$	T	
D.1	Sept. '74– Nov. '13	470	-3.525	8.663 (1.049)		.080 (.012) [.025]			.800 (.139)	14.876 (1.193)		.416 (.111)		.664
D.2	Sept. '74– Nov. '13	470	1.052		-1.250 (.309)	.128 (.011) [.025]			.974 (.148)	14.827 (1.276)		.397 (.117)		.628
D.3	Sept. '74– Nov. '13	470	-4.837	9.426 (.961)		.121 (.012) [.025]			-.058 (.151)		7.873 (.471)	.315 (.102)		.720
D.4	Sept. '74– Nov. '13	470	0.352		-1.615 (.288)	.169 (.011) [.025]			.080 (.154)		7.940 (.512)	.288 (.108)		.683
D.5	Sept. '74– Nov. '13	470	5.186	9.359 (1.038)		.095 (.012) [.025]			.466 (.149)			.396 (.109)		.675
D.6	Sept. '74– Nov. '13	470	10.205		-1.463 (.309)	.144 (.011) [.025]			.647 (.161)			.375 (.116)		.635
D.7	Sept. '74– Nov. '13	470	-0.380	.839 (.434)			.922 (.020)	10.981 (.633)	.009 (.064)	1.000 (.605)			-.015 (.001)	.932
D.8	Sept. '74– Nov. '13	470	0.129		-.174 (.126)		.936 (.018)	11.083 (.630)	.009 (.066)	.784 (.588)				.932
D.9	Sept. '74– Nov. '13	470	-0.762	1.402 (.486)			.907 (.021)	10.798 (.631)	-.072 (.072)		.755 (.254)		-.015 (.001)	.933
D.10	Sept. '74– Nov. '13	470	0.099		-.275 (.135)		.931 (.017)	10.981 (.628)	-.053 (.073)		.555 (.237)			.933

[a] The dependent variable in regressions D.1–D.10 is ρ_t.

measured in terms of percentage rather than arithmetic differences, but this was not attempted. The result for $\Delta\rho_t$ may be due to imperfect approximation to the instantaneous rate of change in ρ_t. The intercorrelations of $\Delta\rho_t$ with other independent variables are relatively low, so that multicollinearity is probably not a factor contributing to its poor performance.

The last four regressions in Table 10, (D.7)–(D.10), represent tests of the lag-in-adjustment model. As the empirical counterpart of $\bar{v}$, we used $\log_e(D\rho_{t+1}/D\rho_{t-1})$. The introduction of ρ_{t-1} as one of the independent variables has a drastic effect on the regression coefficients for other independent variables, reducing their size and their significance, as compared with (D.1)–(D.6). The lagged value of ρ_t by itself explains more than 88 per cent of the variance in ρ_t; the other variables explain about 42 per cent of the remaining variance in ρ_t. The estimated coefficients of ρ_{t-1} and the adjustment coefficients derived from them suggest a shorter lag, in adjustment of desired to actual ρ_t, than was found in estimating the lag in expectations for q_t. The median lag in adjustment, i.e., the number of past months required to obtain half of the weight applied to past periods[4] is 7.5 months in the case of (D.7). In the case of (D.5), the corresponding lag required to account for half the β weights, when $\beta = .025$, is 27.6 months.[5]

How is this discrepancy accounted for? Of course, the lags refer to different models, and even a recasting of the expectations model in difference equation form would not yield the same reduced equation for purposes of estimation. But this is not the heart of the matter. Rather, it would seem that regressions involving lagged values of the dependent variable will tend to produce estimates of the coefficient of the lagged dependent variable which are biased. Griliches and others have suggested that the bias is likely to be upward, owing to the common correlation of both dependent and lagged dependent variables with variables which are relevant but which, for one reason or another, have been omitted from the regression.[6] On the other hand, if the dependent variable is subject to

---

[4] The relevant formula is $n = [\log (1 - Sn)/\log (1 - \gamma)] - 1$, where n is the number of months required for Sn, the sum of the weights for the first n past periods, to equal any arbitrary amount $(0 < Sn \leq 1)$, and γ is the adjustment coefficient (equals one minus the regression coefficient for ρ_{t-1}). See M. Nerlove, *Distributed Lags and Demand Analysis for Agricultural and Other Commodities*, U.S. Department of Agriculture Handbook No. 141 (Washington: U.S. Government Printing Office, 1958), p. 48.

[5] The formula for this median lag is $.69/\beta$. See M. Friedman, *A Theory of the Consumption Function* (New York: National Bureau of Economic Research, 1957), p. 145.

[6] G. E. Barndow, "A Note on the Nerlove Estimate of Supply Elasticity," *Journal of Farm Economics*, XL (August, 1958), 719–22, and Z. Griliches, "Distributed Lags, Disaggregation, and Regional Demand for Fertilizer," *Journal of Farm Economics*, XLI (February, 1959), 90–102.

important errors of measurement, the same will also apply to the lagged dependent variable, so that we are faced with the problem of fitting a regression when both independent and dependent variables are subject to error.[7] As is well known, least squares estimates of the parameters of independent variables subject to error are biased downward under these conditions.[8] But if there is positive serial correlation in the errors of measurement, this bias need not be downward.

B. Tests on Weekly Reporting Member Banks, 1921–51, Tables 11 and 12

Let us now turn to Tables 11 and 12, which report the results of similar tests on data for New York weekly reporting member banks. In Table 11 the time period covered is July, 1921, through November, 1955. Data for weekly reporting banks are available beginning in 1919, but it was decided to exclude observations for months prior to July, 1921.[9] I shall dwell only briefly on Table 11 results because of two defects in the data used in fitting these regressions.[10]

On the whole, regressions (D.11)–(D.20) show results similar to those obtained for New York Clearing House Banks. Regression coefficients for interest rate variables are, with one exception, four or more times their standard errors, while q_t and $\ln (Dp_{t+1}/Dp_{t-1})$ turn out to be highly significant, as does the lagged dependent variable. Also, $B_t - S_t$ shows the same tendency to be significant in equations involving σ_t but not the lagged dependent variable. Again the coefficient for $\Delta \rho_t$ has the wrong sign, but this time its standard error shows it to be non-significant. As before, the introduction of the lagged dependent variable serves to reduce

[7] See, for example, A. Madansky, "The Fitting of Straight Lines When Both Variables Are Subject to Error," *Journal of the American Statistical Association*, LIV (March, 1959), 173–205.

[8] *Ibid.*, p. 177.

[9] Among the reasons for this decision: (a) the report date was Friday before May, 1921, and has been Wednesday since then; (b) before about June, 1921, the "tradition against continuous borrowing" was not emphasized in Federal Reserve administration of the "discount window," so that banks were free to borrow for profit as well as for meeting reserve deficiencies; (c) vault cash displays a strong and steady decline as a percentage of revised deposits (compare Fig. 7 with Fig. 3), particularly before 1921. Probably this decline represents a long-run adjustment to the 1917 amendment under which vault cash no longer counted as part of required reserves. To include the earlier 1919–June, 1921 period in our regressions would lead to biased parameter estimates due to the gradual shift that was taking place.

[10] The defects are, first, that neither ρ_t, ρ_{e_t}, nor the Dp_t series underlying the q_t series were seasonally adjusted for the period January, 1932, through December, 1947, and second, that no adjustment was made for a revision of the weekly reporting series beginning with January, 1952. The revision resulted in only about a 1 per cent increase in the level of the Dp_t series, but it is possible this could have had some effect on the fitting of the q_t series.

TABLE 11

REGRESSIONS, NEW YORK WEEKLY REPORTING BANKS, 1921–55[a]

(Monthly Data)

Equation Number	Period Covered	Number of Observations	Dependent Variable	Constant Term	Coefficients, Standard Errors (in parentheses) of Independent Variables, and β Values of q_t Variables (in brackets)[b]											R^2
					$1/r_t$	$\ln r_t$	q_t	ρ_{t-1}	ρe_{t-1}	$\ln(Dp_{t+1}/Dp_{t-1})$	$B_t - S_t$	σ_t	P_t^q	$\Delta\rho_t$	0 or 1	
D.11	July '21–Nov. '55	413	ρ_t	3.945	.143 (.071)		.196 (.005) [.01]				.522 (.143)	−3.689 (1.003)		.127 (.147)	−2.461 (.323)	.925
D.12	July '21–Nov. '55	413	ρ_t	−0.036	.022 (.000)			.958 (.009)		7.796 (.578)	.061 (.057)	.076 (.040)			−.158 (.133)	.988
D.13	July '21–Nov. '55	413	ρ_t	0.593		−.350 (.082)		.945 (.011)		7.958 (.575)	.289 (.099)	.595 (.427)			−.178 (.134)	.988
D.14	July '21–Nov. '55	413	ρ_t	−0.011	.021 (.005)			.958 (.009)		7.821 (.578)	.057 (.059)		−.110 (.336)		−.174 (.122)	.988
D.15	July '21–Nov. '55	413	ρ_t	0.546		−.384 (.089)		.938 (.001)		7.926 (.575)	.236 (.086)		.652 (.389)		−.241 (.125)	.988
D.16	July '21–Nov. '55	413	ρe_t	2.770	.150 (.011)		.204 (.005) [.01]				.381 (.137)	−1.967 (.950)				.921
D.17	July '21–Nov. '55	413	ρe_t	−0.083	.022 (.005)				.956 (.009)	7.965 (.595)	.080 (.060)	−.010 (.413)			−.150 (.136)	.987
D.18	July '21–Nov. '55	413	ρe_t	0.565		−.370 (.086)			.941 (.012)	8.121 (.592)	.285 (.101)	.518 (.438)			−.173 (.137)	.988
D.19	July '21–Nov. '55	413	ρe_t	−0.057	.022 (.005)				.955 (.009)	7.979 (.595)	.070 (.061)		.130 (.347)		−.156 (.125)	.988
D.20	July '21–Nov. '55	413	ρe_t	0.509		−.402 (.091)			.935 (.013)	8.084 (.592)	.236 (.089)		.622 (.389)		−.222 (.128)	.988

[a] Note that ρ_t, ρe_t, q_t, and Dp_t are not seasonally adjusted, January, 1932–December, 1947.

[b] The q_t series in this table is not necessarily optimal, since no series with β weight of less than .01 was tried.

TABLE 12

Regressions, New York Weekly Reporting Banks, 1921–51[a]

(Monthly Data)

Equation Number	Period Covered	Number of Observations	Dependent Variable	Constant Term	Coefficients, Standard Errors (in parentheses) or Independent Variables, and β Values of q_t Variables (in brackets)[b]										R^2
					$1/r_t$	$\log_e r_t$	$r_t - d_t$	$r_t - p_t$	$B_t - S_t$	P_t^m	d_t	p_t	q_t	T	
D.21	July '21–Dec. '51	366	ρe_t	7.033	.176 (.014)				−2.005 (.339)	1.856 (.234)	−1.576 (.177)		.225 (.008) [.02]		.887
D.22	July '21–Dec. '51	366	ρe_t	5.404	.188 (.014)				−1.298 (.332)	1.424 (.231)		−1.108 (1.64)	.222 (.008) [.02]		.878
D.23	July '21–Dec. '51	366	ρe_t	2.630			−.178 (.309)		.596 (.321)	.417 (.249)			.269 (.009) [.02]		.781
D.24	July '21–Dec. '51	366	ρe_t	3.371				.653 (.335)	.314 (.320)	.236 (.255)			.265 (.009) [.02]		.783
D.25	July '21–Dec. '51	366	ρe_t	7.806		−3.771 (.173)			−3.498 (.265)	.916 (.196)	−.002 (.169)		.165 (.007) [.02]		.929
D.26	July '21–Dec. '51	366	ρe_t	7.556		−3.832 (.161)			−3.388 (.256)	.822 (.180)		.103 (.142)	.163 (.007) [.02]		.929
D.27	July '21–Dec. '51	366	ρe_t	5.021	.176 (.014)				−1.907 (.364)	1.866 (.234)	−1.428 (.267)		.226 (.008) [.02]	.002 (.003)	.888

a Note that ρ_t, ρe_t, and q_t are not seasonally adjusted, December, 1942–December, 1947.

b The q series in this table is not necessarily the optimum, since no series with β weight of less than .02 was tried.

145

TABLE 12—Continued

Coefficients, Standard Errors (in parentheses) of Independent Variables, and β Values of q_t Variables (in brackets)[b]

Equation Number	Period Covered	Number of Observations	Dependent Variable	Constant Term	$1/r_t$	$\log_e r_t$	$r_t - d_t$	$r_t - p_t$	$B_t - S_t$	P^m	d_t	p_t	q_t	T	R^2
D.28	July '21–Dec. '51	366	ρe_t	−0.1740	.186 (.014)					1.488 (.231)		−.582 (.261)	.223 (.008) [.02]	.008 (.003)	.880
D.29	July '21–Dec. '51	366	ρe_t	17.099		−4.236 (.162)			−3.357 (.245)		−.140 (.191)		.148 (.007) [.02]	−.011 (.002)	.929
D.30	July '21–Dec. '51	366	ρe_t	17.606		−4.253 (.161)			−3.400 (.257)			−.172 (.188)	.148 (.007) [.02]	−.011 (.002)	.929
D.31	July '21–Dec. '51	366	ρe_t	−2.957			−.704 (.274)		−.062 (.336)				.272 (.009) [.02]	.010 (.002)	.794
D.32	July '21–Dec. '51	366	ρe_t	−3.586				−1.439 (.296)	−.688 (.344)				.265 (.008) [.02]	.012 (.002)	.803

the explanatory power of the other independent variables. And the estimated adjustment lag again turns out to be substantially less (15.2 months for [D.12]) than the estimated expectations lag (69 months for equation [D.4]).

The only difference in form between the present set of regressions and the earlier ones is the introduction of a dummy variable to reflect the influence of pegging of Treasury bill rates during the period from May, 1942, to August, 1947. Treasury bills were made virtually the equivalent of cash, so that it would be reasonable to expect excess reserves to fall to extremely low levels during this period. The coefficient for the dummy variable has the expected sign and high level of significance in (D.11). But in equations involving lagged dependent variables, it adds nothing, since the lagged dependent variable absorbs nearly all of the shift that would otherwise need to be explained.

In Table 12 several modifications in testing procedure were made. First, it was decided to concentrate on explaining the excess reserve ratio, since for reasons given in footnote 9, page 143, it appeared that the inclusion of vault cash in regressions including data for the early 1920's would possibly bias the results.[11]

Another important change was the replacement of P_t^a by P_t^m. The Macaulay railroad bond yield series, on which P_t^a is based, are not available after January, 1937. The use of P_t^a in the regressions of Table 9 can be justified if it serves as a variable to "purify" the call loan rate of default risk elements. At the point in the r_t series where yields on short governments replace call loan rates as indicators of the cost of holding money, the yield spread between low-grade and high-grade bonds is no longer needed, and is therefore set equal to zero. This happens in January, 1930.[12]

Finally, it was decided to experiment with the discount rate and the federal funds rate as possible measures of the penalty cost of meeting a

[11] I have taken this opportunity to replace seasonally unadjusted series for ρ_{e_t} and $D\rho_t$ with seasonally adjusted series for the period January, 1932, through November, 1942.

At the same time, I elected to drop the observations after December, 1951, to avoid possible errors arising from the use of data unadjusted for the revision in weekly reporting bank data beginning in January, 1952. As indicated in Appendix C, the weekly reporting series for New York banks has, in the last decade or so, become less satisfactory for our purposes, so that the decision to drop the last four years of data seemed desirable on grounds other than expediency.

[12] But it is also possible to view this spread as representing the default risk characteristics of the bank's asset portfolio in the much broader sense outlined in Chapter II—in which case, a variable such as P_t^m (which can be measured for the entire period of investigation) might be retained.

cash deficiency. In the p_t series, the discount rate is used wherever the federal funds rate is unavailable or inoperative, as apparently it was during much of the 1930's and 1940's.[13] Both p_t and d_t series are set equal to zero for the period of pegged Treasury bill rates, on the grounds that a deficiency could then be met at zero cost by sale of Treasury bills to the Federal Reserve.[14]

Once again, the interest rate variables and q_t stand out as the most successful explanatory factors, with the risk premium, P_t^m, running a fairly close third. The failure of the $B_t - S_t$, d_t, and p_t coefficients to display the correct sign with any consistency is partly due to the rather high inter-correlations among these variables (and among $\log_e r_t$, $r_t - d_t$, and $r_t - p_t$ as well). Multicollinearity may have affected the parameter estimates for $B_t - S_t$ more, inasmuch as the simple correlation between ρ_{e_t} and $B_t - S_t$ is +.41, whereas the partial correlations with two exceptions, turn out to be negative.

The outcome of the experiments reported in Tables 11 and 12 suggest that of the factors tested, the three most important influences on bank demand for excess cash reserves are short-term interest rates, default risk, and transitory deposit potential. This is in accord with our earlier results for New York Clearing House Banks.

C. Subperiod Tests on Weekly Reporting Banks, 1921–30 and 1948–51, Tables 13 to 16

Tables 13 to 16 report a number of regressions run on the separate subperiods, 1921–30 (Tables 13 and 14) and 1948–51 (Tables 15 and 16). In the 1921–30 tests, the only variables which consistently show significance are q_t and $\log_e(Dp_{t+1}/Dp_{t-1})$; even the lagged dependent variable $\rho_{e_{t-1}}$ fails to help explain movements of ρ_{e_t} in (D.45)–(D.48). In (D.35)–(D.36) and (D.43)–(D.44), the interest rate and the risk premium, P_t^a, show somewhat greater strength, but because of the strong trend element in the movement of ρ_t during the 1920's, little confidence can be placed in this result. The poor over-all performances of the interest rate and risk premium cannot be attributed to multicollinearity; inter-correlations of $1/r_t$, $\log_e r_t$, and P_t^a, with other independent variables are generally not great. The one exception is a high correlation between interest rates and $B_t - S_t$. But omission of $B_t - S_t$ does not improve matters.

[13] U.S., Board of Governors of the Federal Reserve System, *The Federal Funds Market* (Washington: Board of Governors, 1959), pp. 29–30.

[14] The Federal Reserve stood ready to buy or sell bills at a yield of three-eights of 1 per cent per annum.

TABLE 13

REGRESSIONS, NEW YORK BANKS, 1921–30

(Monthly Data)

EQUATION NUMBER	TIME PERIOD COVERED	NUMBER OF OBSERVATIONS	DEPENDENT VARIABLE	CONSTANT TERM	COEFFICIENTS, STANDARD ERRORS (IN PARENTHESES) OF INDEPENDENT VARIABLES, AND β VALUES OF q_t VARIABLES (IN BRACKETS)										R^2
					$1/r_t$	$\log_e r_t$	q_t	ρ_{t-1}	ρq_{t-1}	$\log_e(D\rho_{t+1}/D\rho_{t-1})$	$B_t - S_t$	σ_t	P_t^a	$\Delta \rho_t$	
D.33	July '21–Dec. '30	114	ρ_t	0.770	−1.515 (.400)	……	.108 (.014) [.80]	……	……	……	.118 (.052)	10.051 (.482)	……	−.129 (.129)	.836
D.34	July '21–Dec. '30	114	ρ_t	0.032	……	.293 (.165)	.105 (.014) [.80]	……	……	……	.069 (.076)	10.322 (.500)	……	−.177 (.135)	.820
D.35	July '21–Dec. '30	114	ρ_t	0.810	.945 (.359)	……	.091 (.011) [.80]	……	……	……	−.093 (.045)	……	2.678 (.010)	−.015 (.108)	.886
D.36	July '21–Dec. '30	114	ρ_t	1.676	……	−.391 (.133)	.092 (.011) [.80]	……	……	……	−.155 (.061)	……	2.625 (.096)	−.013 (.107)	.888
D.37	July '21–Dec. '30	114	ρe_t	0.356	−.379 (.268)	……	.108 (.009) [.80]	……	……	……	.070 (.035)	.443 (.327)	……	……	.584
D.38	July '21–Dec. '30	114	ρe_t	0.196	……	.051 (.107)	.107 (.009) [.80]	……	……	……	.048 (.049)	.516 (.325)	……	……	.577
D.39	July '21–Dec. '30	114	ρe_t	0.340	−.215 (.289)	……	.107 (.009) [.80]	……	……	……	.054 (.037)	……	.154 (.083)	……	.590

TABLE 13—Continued

COEFFICIENTS, STANDARD ERRORS (IN PARENTHESES) OF INDEPENDENT VARIABLES, AND β VALUES OF q_t VARIABLES (IN BRACKETS)

EQUATION NUMBER	TIME PERIOD COVERED	NUMBER OF OBSERVATIONS	DEPENDENT VARIABLE	CONSTANT TERM	$1/r_t$	$\log_e r_t$	q_t	ρ_{t-1}	ρ_{q-1}	$\log_e(Dp_{t+1}/Dp_{t-1})$	$B_t - S_t$	σ_t	P_t^a	$\Delta\rho_t$	R^2
D.40....	July '21– Dec. '30	114	ρe_t	0.297		.0007 (.108)	.106 (.009) [.80]				.030 (.050)		.180 (.077)		.588
D.41....	July '21– Dec. '30	114	ρ_t	0.402	−.790 (.436)			.447 (.078)		2.194 (.510)	.061 (.056)	5.411 (.960)			.818
D.42....	July '21– Dec. '30	114	ρ_t	−0.061		.172 (.169)		.476 (.076)		2.176 (.518)	.044 (.078)	5.247 (.964)			.814
D.43....	July '21– Dec. '30	114	ρ_t	0.585	.813 (.438)			.222 (.092)		1.646 (.492)	−.071 (.054)		2.075 (.291)		.840
D.44....	July '21– Dec. '30	114	ρ_t	1.269		−.301 (.165)		.221 (.093)		1.649 (.492)	−.108 (.074)		2.027 (.282)		.840
D.45....	July '21– Dec. '30	114	ρe_t	0.252	−.243 (.385)				.141 (.098)	1.593 (.490)	.070 (.051)	.361 (.471)			.158
D.46....	July '21– Dec. '30	114	ρe_t	0.140		.038 (.153)			.142 (.098)	1.573 (.492)	.058 (.071)	.407 (.465)			.156
D.47....	July '21– Dec. '30	114	ρe_t	0.228	−.062 (.416)				.122 (.099)	1.536 (.490)	.054 (.053)		.160 (.122)		.167
D.48....	July '21– Dec. '30	114	ρe_t	0.235		−.011 (.156)			.122 (.099)	1.521 (.490)	.042 (.071)		.170 (.113)		.167

150

TABLE 14

REGRESSIONS, NEW YORK BANKS, 1921-30

(Monthly Data)

Equation Number	Time Period Covered	Number of Observations	Dependent Variable	Constant Term	Coefficients, Standard Errors (in parentheses) of Independent Variables, and β Values of q_t Variables (in brackets)									R^2
					$1/r_t$	$\log g_t$	$r_t - d_t$	$r_t - p_t$	$B_t - S_t$	P_t^m	d_t	p_t	q_t	
D.49......	July '21–Dec. '30	114	ρe_t	0.639	$-.495$ (.265)	......	......	......	.024 (.047)	.065 (.031)	$-.065$ (.041)	......	.111 (.009) [.80]	.594
D.50......	July '21–Dec. '30	114	ρe_t	0.247	$-.379$ (.276)	......	......	......	.098 (.045)	.024 (.029)	......	.026 (.034)	.107 (.009) [.80]	.587
D.51......	July '21–Dec. '30	114	ρe_t	0.286	......	......	.004 (.020)	......	.029 (.025)	.038 (.028)	......	......	.106 (.009) [.80]	.574
D.52......	July '21–Dec. '30	114	ρe_t	0.346	......	......	......	$-.025$ (.021)	.006 (.023)	.020 (.028)	......	......	.106 (.009) [.80]	.580
D.53......	July '21–Dec. '30	114	ρe_t	0.372	......	.095 (.109)	......	......	.011 (.057)	.065 (.031)	$-.061$ (.041)	......	.109 (.009) [.80]	.584
D.54......	July '21–Dec. '30	114	ρe_t	0.102	......	.020 (.116)	......	......	.075 (.054)	.020 (.029)	......	.037 (.036)	.106 (.009) [.80]	.580

TABLE 15
Regressions, New York Weekly Reporting Banks, 1948–51
(Monthly Data)

Equation Number	Time Period Covered	Number of Observations	Dependent Variable	Constant Term	Coefficients, Standard Errors (in parentheses) of Independent Variables, and β Values of q_t Variables (in brackets)							R^2
					$1/r_t$	$\log s_t$	q_t	ρ_{t-1}	ρ_{N-1}	$\log_e (Dp_{t+1}/Dp_{t-1})$	$B_t - S_t$	
D.55	Feb. '48– Mar. '51	38	ρ_t	−0.615	2.089 (.565)	......	.345 (.059) [.70]	......	......	......	.320 (.269)	.535
D.56	Feb. '48– Mar. '51	38	ρ_t	1.443	......	−1.708 (.459)	.313 (.053) [.60]	......	......	......	.332 (.269)	.538
D.57	Feb. '48– Dec. '51	47	ρe_t	−1.529	2.374 (.510)	......	.311 (.048) [.60]	......	......	......	.246 (.243)	.598
D.58	Feb. '48– Dec. '51	47	ρe_t	0.835	......	−1.958 (.415)	.317 (.048) [.60]	......	......	......	.233 (.243)	.602
D.59	Feb. '48– Mar. '51	38	ρ_t	−0.268	.571 (.795)	......	......	.357 (.171)	......	4.547 (3.423)	.534 (.381)	.198
D.60	Feb. '48– Mar. '51	38	ρ_t	0.295	......	− .483 (.649)	......	.361 (.169)	......	4.683 (3.479)	.533 (.380)	.199
D.61	Feb. '48– Dec. '51	47	ρe_t	−0.809	.696 (.770)	......	......	......	.391 (.170)	4.251 (3.235)	.466 (.365)	.237
D.62	Feb. '48– Dec. '51	47	ρe_t	−0.121	......	− .588 (.625)	......	......	.395 (.168)	4.419 (3.285)	.465 (.363)	.238

152

TABLE 16

REGRESSIONS, NEW YORK WEEKLY REPORTING BANKS, 1948–51

(Monthly Data)

EQUATION NUMBER	TIME PERIOD COVERED	NUMBER OF OBSERVATIONS	DEPENDENT VARIABLE	CONSTANT TERM	COEFFICIENTS, STANDARD ERRORS (IN PARENTHESES) OF INDEPENDENT VARIABLES, AND β VALUES OF q_t VARIABLES (IN BRACKETS)									R^2
					$1/r_t$	$\log_e r_t$	q_t	$B_t - S_t$	P_t^m	d_t	p_t	$r_t - d_t$	$r_t - p_t$	
D.63	Feb. '48–Dec. '51	47	ρ_t	1.345	−1.011 (.639)	....	.212 (.040) [.60]	.192 (.287)	1.645 (.471)	−.700 (.497)	....	....	....	.498
D.64	Feb. '48–Dec. '51	47	ρ_t	−0.661	−.166 (.480)	....	.197 (.039) [.60]	.360 (.267)	1.519 (.481)	....	.110 (.145)	....	....	.481
D.65	Feb. '48–Dec. '51	47	ρ_t	−0.554	....	....	.212 (.035) [.60]	.275 (.209)	1.784 (.413)	....	....	.685 (.305)	....	.524
D.66	Feb. '48–Dec. '51	47	ρ_t	−0.398	....	....	.196 (.038) [.60]	.235 (.220)	1.328 (.399)	....	....	....	−.046 (.140)	.467
D.67	Feb. '48–Dec. '51	47	ρ_t	0.444	....	.892 (.448)	.216 (.039) [.60]	.197 (.283)	1.701 (.457)	−.801 (.475)	....	....	....	.514
D.68	Feb. '48–Dec. '51	47	ρ_t	−0.938	....	.239 (.347)	.194 (.038) [.60]	.402 (.265)	1.607 (.473)	....	.090 (.143)	....	....	.485

A similar picture is presented in Tables 15 and 16, for the 1948–51 period. Transitory deposit potential continues to show significance, and P_t^m is also a consistent performer in regressions (D.63)–(D.68). Only when P_t^m is omitted, as in regressions (D.55)–(D.58), does the short-term interest rate show to advantage. And once again, the equations involving lagged dependent values of ρ_{e_t} produce poor results.

APPENDIX E

Spurious Correlation

As has been pointed out by Meyer and Kuh, there is nothing wrong with correlating two ratios containing a common element if, as in our model, there is a good theoretical basis for preferring ratio comparisons to comparisons of absolutes,[1] and if the common element has been measured without error. There are few instances, however, in which the latter condition is met, and ours is not one of them.

The way in which correlation of common elements enters into our regressions and correlations can be seen most clearly in the computations of ρ_t and q_t under the regulations applicable under the national banking system. Let R_t denote total reserves (specie and legal tender), D_t denote total deposits subject to reserve, and M_t denote the volume of national banknotes outstanding. Then the excess cash reserve ratio is calculated as

$$\rho_t = \frac{R_t - .25D_t + .05M_t}{D_t - .25D_t} = \frac{R_t - .25D_t + .05M_t}{.75D_t}, \quad (E.1)$$

where .25 and .05 are, respectively, the required reserve ratio against D_t and the redemption fund requirement as a ratio to M_t. On the other hand, q_t is computed as

$$q_t = \frac{D p_t}{E_t} - 1 = \frac{D p_t}{\xi D p_t + \Psi E_{t-1}} - 1 = \frac{\dfrac{R_t}{.25}}{\dfrac{\xi R_t + \Psi R_{t-1}^*}{.25}} - 1$$

$$= \frac{R_t}{\xi R_t + \Psi R_{t-1}^*} - 1, \quad (E.2)$$

where $\xi = \beta/(\beta - a)(1 - e^{a-\beta})$ and $\Psi = e^{a-\beta}$ (see Appendix A, *supra*,) and denotes R_{t-1}^* expected reserves for period $t - 1$. It can be seen that errors

---

[1] E. Kuh and J. R. Meyer, "Correlation and Regression Estimates When Data Are Ratios," *Econometrica*, XXIII (October, 1955), 400–416. Also see K. Pearson, "On a Form of Spurious Correlation Which May Arise When Indices Are Used in the Measurement of Organs," *Proceedings of the Royal Statistical Society of London*, LX (1897), 489 ff.

of measurement in R_t will tend to produce a positive but spurious correlation between ρ_t and q_t.[2]

The problem of spurious correlation in this form has received scant attention in the literature, and I have been unable to come up with anything very precise regarding the degree to which such spurious correlation weakens the results I have reported. One's natural inclination is to minimize its importance, and the following considerations should be received in that light.

The first of these considerations has to do with the effect of seasonal adjustment. Although there is no necessary reason why seasonal adjustment should reduce the degree of common measurement error, it would appear likely that it did, in fact, do so in this case. My approach was to seasonally adjust $D p_t$ and ρ_t (where ρ_t had an arbitrary 100 per cent added to it). As compared with a procedure in which the variables R_t, D_t, and M_t underlying the calculation of ρ_t by (E.1) would each be seasonally adjusted, the approach that was taken operates to reduce the importance of common measurement errors.

Spurious correlation between ρ_{e_t} and q_t is less than between ρ_t and q_t, not only because the error in measurement of vault cash does not enter into the calculation of ρ_{e_t}, as it does in calculating ρ_t and q_t, but also be-

---

[2] The corresponding q_t and ρ_t formulas for weekly reporting banks are: (1) for the periods, January, 1919–August, 1935, and April, 1943–June, 1947:

$$\rho_t = \frac{R_t - \chi D_t - \Omega J_t}{D_t + J_t + G_t - \chi D_t - \Omega J_t} \tag{E.3}$$

and

$$q_t = \frac{\dfrac{R_t(D_t + J_t)}{\chi D_t + \Omega J_t}}{\xi\left[\dfrac{R_t(D_t + J_t)}{\chi D_t + \Omega J_t}\right] + \Psi E_{t-1}} - 1, \tag{E.4}$$

where D_t now denotes net demand deposits subject to reserve, J_t denotes time deposits, and G_t denotes U.S. government demand deposits. The reserve requirements against demand and time deposits are, respectively, χ and Ω. (2) For the periods, September, 1935–March, 1943, and July, 1947–December, 1955:

$$\rho_t = \frac{R_t - \chi(D_t + G_t) - \Omega J_t}{D_t + J_t + G_t - \chi(D_t + G_t) - \Omega J_t} \tag{E.5}$$

and

$$q_t = \frac{\dfrac{R_t(D_t + J_t + G_t)}{\chi(D_t + G_t) + \Omega J_t}}{\xi\left[\dfrac{R_t(D_t + J_t + G_t)}{\chi(D_t + G_t)\Omega + J_t}\right] + \Psi E_{t-1}} - 1. \tag{E.6}$$

cause ρ_{e_t} was seasonally adjusted by the Census Method II programed for the IBM 650, whereas q_t was seasonally adjusted by the Univac programed Method II. Comparisons have shown that the two variants of Method II differ somewhat in the seasonally adjusted series they produce.

The tenor of the foregoing observations is that there are several factors tending to create errors of measurement which are not likely to be correlated, so that on this ground alone the observed correlation between ρ_t and q_t would tend to be less than the true correlation.[3] In addition to seasonal adjustment, the presence of other variables subject to measurement error (Dp_t, R^*_{t-1}, and M_t) operate in such a way as to offset the upward bias in the observed correlation that arises from variables with common errors.

Another argument tending to downgrade the significance of spurious correlation of measurement errors is that of Briggs.[4] He examines the relation between the true and observed correlations between x/y and x, y/x and z/x, and x/y and z/x under three different situations: (a) linear correlation and additive errors in x only; (b) linear correlation and multiplicative uniformly distributed errors in x only; and (c) logarithmic correlation and multiplicative errors in x only. He is able in the majority of these cases to derive formulas for the bias in the observed correlation that depend only on observed statistics and assumptions about the relative size of the variance in the measurement error. By application of the formulas to specific sets of economic data, Briggs concludes from his results that "in none of the cases examined was the effect of the observation errors sufficient to give rise to misleading correlations."[5] One of the cases, however, which proved intractable to analysis is the one most similar to our problem—linear correlation of y/x and z/x when there are additive errors in x.

But even if the spurious element in the correlation between ρ_t and q_t does not impart a substantial upward bias to the correlation, it may still be sufficient to bias significantly the statistical determination of the "best" β-weighted q_t series. By the argument of the preceding paragraph, the tendency will be for the errors of measurement to be more influential the smaller is the variance of the denominator of the q_t ratio. This variance

---

[3] See G. U. Yule and M. G. Kendall, *An Introduction to the Theory of Statistics* (13th ed. [rev.]; London: Charles Griffin & Co., 1949), p. 298.

[4] F. E. A. Briggs, "The Influence of Errors on the Correlation of Ratios," *Econometrica*, XXX (January, 1962), 162–77.

[5] *Ibid.*, 175.

will be small when the weight assigned to the current value of potential deposits is also small, i.e., when β is small. It is likely, therefore, that our estimates of the best β weighted q_t series are biased toward series with small β weights. This means that our fitting procedure tends to overestimate the past time period which banks take into account in forming their expectations of "permanent" deposit potential.

Index